JORDANETICS

BOOKS BY VOX DAY

NON FICTION

SJWs Always Lie: Taking Down the Thought Police
SJWs Always Double Down: Anticipating the Thought Police
Cuckservative: How "Conservatives" Betrayed America
(with John Red Eagle)
On the Existence of Gods (with Dominic Saltarelli)
On the Question of Free Trade (with James D. Miller)
The Return of the Great Depression
The Irrational Atheist

ARTS OF DARK AND LIGHT

Summa Elvetica: A Casuistry of the Elvish Controversy
A Throne of Bones
A Sea of Skulls

QUANTUM MORTIS

A Man Disrupted (with Steve Rzasa)
Gravity Kills (with Steve Rzasa)
A Mind Programmed (with Jeff and Jean Sutton)

ETERNAL WARRIORS

The War in Heaven
The World in Shadow
The Wrath of Angels

COLLECTIONS

The Altar of Hate
Riding the Red Horse Vol. 1 (ed. with Tom Kratman)

Foreword by Milo Yiannopoulos

JORDANETICS

A JOURNEY INTO THE MIND OF HUMANITY'S GREATEST THINKER

VOX DAY

CASTALIA HOUSE

Jordanetics: A Journey Into the Mind of Humanity's Greatest Thinker

Vox Day

Published by Castalia House
Kouvola, Finland
www.castaliahouse.com

Cover: Steve Beaulieu

ISBN: 9789527065693
Version: 006

Contents

Foreword: The Two Types of Chameleon

I'm a smart person. Really smart, actually, and very expensively educated! But half the time, I just can't understand a bloody word Jordan Peterson says. And I've been thinking recently about why that could be. Ordinarily, I can listen to someone prattling on and quickly get to the heart of what they are trying to express. That's one of the skills you pick up as a journalist: You learn to quickly identify the core of a problem, the essence of what's being said. You learn to filter out the noise—and to identify bullshitters. But with Jordan Peterson, once I've filtered out the noise, I don't find a lot left to work with. And there's another problem. He lies.

When he first began to speak about me, Jordan Peterson described me as "an amazing person." This was around the time he called me on the telephone, expressing sympathy for the failed assassination attempt on me in February 2017, when I was wrongly accused of supporting child rapists. He offered to do a series of on-camera interviews with me. He described me publicly, and correctly, as "a trickster figure," explaining that "trickster figures emerge in times of crisis. And they point out what no one wants to see. And they say things that no one will say …

He continued: "[Milo's] brave as can be…. And he's unstoppable on his feet. He just amazes me. I've never seen anyone I don't think—and I've met some pretty smart people—I've never seen anyone who can take on an onslaught of criticism and reverse it like he can." Fast-forward to

JORDANETICS

an on-stage interview with Bari Weiss in June 2018 at the Aspen Ideas Festival. Weiss is talking about about a professor who paired me with Hitler and gave us as examples of Very Bad Things. She alleges that I, the interracially married man, am indeed a racist.

To which Peterson replies: "Well, possibly, yeah … I haven't followed Milo that carefully."

What happened? By his own definition, this is the way demagogues work: by listening to their audience and adjusting their responses accordingly. Why was Peterson suddenly going along with something he knew wasn't true and rewriting history, pretending he didn't know that much at all about someone he had on numerous occasions so intelligently explained? I realize that by asking this question, this you're going to think I'm just wounded that someone I once admired has since soured on me. But that's the thing. From the first time I heard Jordan Peterson speak, my nostrils picked up a whiff of sulfur in the air—and not just because he dresses in that awful, drab, monotonous Victoriana.

In an era of social justice, we are desperate to hear people defending Western civilization, and doing so forcefully in a way that shows up the progressive Left for the vacuous, parasitical bullies they are. Men, in particular, need superheroes like never before in history, although they like slightly feminized men, like the products of the Marvel universe, so that even when immersed in their masculine fantasies, they are still the biggest dog in the room. There's nothing less intimidating, or more gay, than the aggressively hypermasculine Thor, the tongue-tied and slightly dim Captain America or Loki, the wily trickster.

Likewise, by presenting himself as an avuncular, asexual, physically frail character, Peterson can be a hero to men without threatening their manhood, much in the same way my homosexuality has also made me a hero to straight men. This is why Peterson has been able to bamboozle some quite clever people into thinking he is the Second Coming. But I have no patience for gobbledygook, and I have no faith in people who, when push comes to shove, will bend for popularity, comfort and an easy life rather than defend what they know to be true.

Peterson's manner of speaking is designed to be fascinating. It's easy to get sucked in. He constantly defers solutions, leaving listeners to fill in the gaps and reach the ultimate conclusions themselves. And he's always hedging his own statements with phrases such as, "It's something like that." The way he speaks is designed to conjure up a rigorously precise, intellectually humble professor who doesn't want to commit wholly to a claim unless he knows he is absolutely correct.

I do not find this way of speaking fascinating, though clearly I'm in the minority. I prefer plain talk. I like simple, clear, unambiguous statements of opinion. I believe in objective truth and such a thing as right and wrong. I'm never going to be satisfied by a writer who is constantly pointing to deeper solutions that are endlessly deferred. I want to know what a person really thinks. I have no idea what Jordan Peterson really thinks.

And I've come to the conclusion that all this constant prevarication occurs not because he's a great teacher, eagerly hoping his charges will make the final leap of their own volition. Nor is it because he's a modest Socratic thinker. No. It's a public relations strategy, deployed so he never really has to commit to saying what he means, because he doesn't really *want* to be understood, because, like his friends in the risible "intellectual dark web," he doesn't actually like or agree with his own fan base. When Peterson is put to the test, he has an established pattern of going soft at the critical moment.

Peterson's watershed was a tweet he must now bitterly regret sending, because it gave the game away entirely. He said Brett Kavanaugh should accept his Supreme Court nomination and then quit. Peterson, apparently forgetting everything he knew about the feral Left, claimed that this might somehow soothe the activist wing of the Democrat Party into treating the rest of us with a bit more civility. Ugh, come off it. I remember thinking to myself, *Jordan Peterson of all people cannot possibly believe this.* And no amount of thrashing around on social media afterwards, claiming he was just engaging in a thought experiment, has persuaded anyone that he was just floating an idea out there.

Peterson's reaction to Kavanaugh raises questions about his attitude to, and relationships with, women, which I haven't seen many people discuss. There is something off about the way he talks about his daughter, though I can't work out what it is. And I note in his habit of describing the feminine as Chaos and the masculine as Order a kind of incomprehension and fear of women, which makes him a very poor role model for men. It does explain his appeal to a certain kind of socially awkward, sexually confused guy, who cannot relate to girls. But Peterson is just the same! So he isn't going to help these guys.

There *is* such a thing as the Chaotic feminine Peterson recognizes. She is the Whore of Babylon, rather than the Heavenly Bride. But Jordan only sees the Whore. This is a fundamental failing in his mythological structure: he doesn't see the Ordering Feminine—the Lady as Heavenly City who gives a home to her groom. Men are constantly asking feminists to be more honest about male virtue. They have to do women the same courtesy. Peterson doesn't, and can't.

What really annoys everyone is how, when the going gets tough, Peterson chucks out everything he's been preaching for the past two years and takes the easy route. He tells his followers to read Solzhenitsyn. He says he knows and hates Marxism. But then he tweets: "If confirmed Kavanaugh should step down." With these six words, he revealed his true strategy in the face of the enemy. Surrender and appeasement. A light knock and this guy dents like a tin can, warping and distorting himself to evade critique.

Peterson and I are sometimes compared with respect to our intellectual dexterity, and I think I understand the root of this misunderstanding. It seems to me that there are two types of chameleon. The first kind uses different modes, styles, fashions, media and mannerisms to convey, to different audiences at different times, the same essential truth. His message does not change, but he is intelligent enough to know that you cannot talk to everyone the same way. These chameleons are charming, adaptable and endlessly insightful about human nature. Politicians who reflexively modify their accents in different parts of the country are of this type.

These chameleons are sometimes wrongly thought of as insubstantial by people with no imagination, subtlety or grasp of humor or artistic license. I have always aspired to be such a thinker and performer, which is why I tell fat jokes and call people cunts during lectures about religion and political philosophy. I enjoy blending highbrow analysis with *sermo humilis* in unexpected and uncomfortable ways, and I don't mind being misunderstood by dullards or misrepresented by snakes. It's the price of being someone as comfortable with billionaires as he is with steelworkers.

But then there is the chameleon who looks and sounds the same all the time, but who adjusts and even completely subverts his own ideology, depending on the audience. Jordan Peterson's grim, predictable wardrobe, his effete speaking style, his pained expressions and his eternally somber affect give the superficial impression of gravity and consistency. But when you look at what he says, you find a coiled and poisonous serpent beneath the dusty carapace.

Asked to define something—anything—Peterson dodges. The author of this book, Vox Day, has suggested that this is the mark of a charlatan. But I see something even worse. There is a theological horror in Peterson's starting position. He believes that life is suffering, which holds only if you define reality purely in terms of pleasure and pain. This is an Enlightenment reduction of truth to what can be proven empirically, carving the world up into claims of value and claims of fact, relegating religion to the realm of the unknowable. As a Catholic, I believe in the objective truth of God's existence and love. But for Peterson, religion lives in the world of subjective feelings, divorced from anything besides the relief of suffering. It thus becomes the opiate of the masses.

Meaning is entirely subjective for Peterson, because he accepts this Enlightenment distinction. That's why he talks about religion as though it were a sort of psychic medicine. And, critically, that's why he's a Marxist—even though he claims to hate Marxism. He believes in the end to which Marx tends, and only hates Marx because Marxism fails to get us there. This is why Peterson's discussions with Sam Harris are so boring. He can't get past trying to make Harris agree that evil is the same as suffering. Marxism is the unkeepable promise of a release from suffering by earthly means, and this is Peterson's entire project.

When he's limiting himself to Tony Robbins-style self-help, Peterson's prescriptions won't do you any harm. Cleaning your room isn't a good habit to get into because there's something intrinsically good about clean rooms. Rather, good practical habits grow into good personal discipline. Most skills develop by increment, not leap. But he can't be trusted to talk about anything that matters. When Peterson reads "When You Wish Upon A Star" as a way of focusing on a transcendent goal, he isn't exactly wrong, but he does not himself believe in the reality of the transcendent. He just wants to fix your mood in the here and now, like a hit of sugar or a compliment from an attractive stranger. He is a line of coke masquerading as the Eucharist.

As Owen Benjamin first noticed, Jordan Peterson has entered what we might call a late decadent phase, in which the bauble of representation by CAA and the promise of stardom act as crucibles, hastening his exposure as Antichrist and diluting his speech and opinions so they are more acceptable to his enemies. He has handed responsibility for his future over to people dedicated to his annihilation. In doing so, he risks us all. Peterson's position and fandom must become untenable. As he himself puts it, in his *12 Rules for Life*, "If the gap between pretense and reality goes unmentioned, it will widen, you will fall into it, and the consequences will not be good. Ignored reality manifests itself in an abyss of confusion and suffering."

If this ruthless careerism comes as a surprise, perhaps you haven't been paying attention. Remember Faith Goldy? She was booted from a conference line-up by Peterson, who un-personed his fellow panelist with a classic mealy-mouthed non-explanation, insinuating that she was "too hot a property." Goldy has made some mistakes, appearing on podcasts with unsavory characters. I would not personally appear on the *Daily Stormer* podcast, especially not in the wake of Charlottesville. But she is not, as far as I can tell, a racist. Peterson himself said, "I don't believe she's a reprehensible person." But he went ahead and killed her career anyway.

Peterson made her untouchable—*persona non grata*—and he did so knowing what the consequences to her life would be. After all, if you're too much for the "extreme" Jordan Peterson, you must really be beyond the pale, right? Goldy has since been physically assaulted by protesters as Canadian media companies sat back and filmed. She has been scrubbed from every online payment service, making it impossible for her to support herself. Ads for her Toronto mayoral campaign have been banned by Rogers and Bell Media. Her life has been destroyed. By Jordan Peterson. She is shouted at in public and assaulted in the street while he tours the world, showered in riches and acclaim.

Peter denied Jesus, just as his nominative descendent Peterson has denied me and others. Both Peters did it for the same reason: fear and self-interest. I don't think it's a coincidence that Peterson denied me in Aspen, in front of what must have been the wealthiest audience he'd ever addressed. And I don't think it's a coincidence that his greatest tell to date happened in relation to a Supreme Court announcement, the most important political event outside of a presidential election. When the chips are down, Peterson goes splat.

I can take inconsistency in people—I am myself a contradictory figure. The pop stars and writers I admire are all complex people. And I can take a degree of studied ambiguity. I see and appreciate the strategy in remaining enigmatic and mysterious, even if it's not to my personal taste in a public intellectual. That doesn't mean I don't enjoy satire or subtlety, obviously—just that I like them in someone who is also capable, when called upon, of calling a spade a spade.

I don't even mind people whose positions and language soften when the establishment offers them fame and wealth in exchange for spaying them. I think it's craven, but I understand now, as a happily married man, why someone might pick comfort and family security over being wholly true to themselves. What I can't tolerate in a public figure is hypocritical disloyalty, the sort of cowardice that hurls allies to the ground in violation of every principle a person has previously stated and in defiance of the very reason the speaker has a platform in the first place. I find Jordan Peterson guilty of this charge, and I cannot excuse it.

If you betray one friend, you will later betray others. If you sacrifice one principle, you cannot be trusted not to sacrifice them all. I have paid a terrible professional and personal price for remaining true to my beliefs and refusing to back down or apologize, unlike some diminutive people I could mention—unsurprisingly, friends with Peterson—who condemned Donald Trump before unctuously praising him a year later for money and popularity. So have other friends of mine in media, politics and academia who know where the slippery slope of moral compromise leads, and who refuse to be soiled by it.

So I know what it looks like, and what it takes out of a person, when he sticks to his guns, no matter the cost. I'm inspired by the fortitude of Pamela Geller and Tommy Robinson, and lucky to call them friends. I am not inspired by Jordan Peterson. Quite aside from the dark, miserable heart of his philosophy, Peterson has repeatedly betrayed everything he says he believes in for his own expediency, convenience and profit, at precisely the time it matters most, and then lied about it all. And that's why I'm glad Vox Day has written this book.

When it really comes down to it, Peterson preaches—and practices—capitulation to the violent delights of feminine Chaos. He isn't prepared to accept the costs of victory or the burden of heroism. He does not hold fast to fact, reason and logic in the face of the maelstrom because he does not possess the heroic manly virtue of courage. The orderliness, certainty and strength of manhood isn't enough to quiet his troubled soul. At a minute to midnight, with the hounds on his tail, Peterson chooses… to believe all women.

Milo Yiannopoulos
Miami, Florida
October 2018

Introduction: The Meandering Fog of Meaning

Be extremely subtle, even to the point of formlessness. Be extremely mysterious, even to the point of soundlessness. Thereby you can be the director of the opponent's fate.

—Sun Tzu

I initially paid no attention to Jordan Peterson's rise. To the extent that I thought of him at all, I assumed he was merely another self-help guru in much the same mode as Deepak Chopra or Tony Robbins, just to name two massively successful self-help authors of the past. But over the last two years, his name kept coming up more and more often in the online circles in which I travel, mostly as a result of his seemingly staunch opposition to the social justice warriors who were the focus of two of my books on political philosophy, *SJWs Always Lie* and *SJWs Always Double Down*.

So, like many others, I assumed that the Canadian professor was one of those rare intellectuals inclined to stand up for the uncomfortable truth in the vein of my friends Milo Yiannopoulos, Mike Cernovich, Ivan Throne, and Stefan Molyneux, without ever actually looking into anything he was writing, saying, or doing. I neither read his work nor wrote about him at all; a single link to a pedestrian interview with him in December 2016 by Canadian journal *C2C* was one of the few times my blog even mentioned him prior to my first direct encounter with the greatest thinker in human history.

On April 24, 2018, Jordan Peterson published an article entitled "On the so-called 'Jewish Question'". In it, he attacked the far right, and labeled its members pathological anti-Semites and "reactionary conspiracy theorists" for their thought crime of offering a rational explanation for what Peterson himself admitted was the over-representation of Jews "in positions of authority, competence and influence."

Because I happen to be a moderately well-known member of the Nationalist Right and the author of the 16 Points of the Nationalist Right, a number of my fellow right-wingers brought the article to my attention and asked me to take a look at it. So I did, and was extremely surprised by what I discovered, in light of how I had hitherto heard only superlatives regarding the man, his intellectual integrity, and his fearless dedication to the truth.

What I was astonished to observe was that Jordan Peterson didn't even bother to consider the vast majority of the relevant evidence available before leaping to what I knew was a wildly erroneous and deeply flawed conclusion. He wrote:

> *No conspiracy. Get it? No conspiracy. Jewish people are over-represented in positions of competence and authority because, as a group, they have a higher mean IQ.... There is no evidence whatsoever that Ashkenazi Jews are over-represented in any occupations/interests for reasons other than intelligence and the associated effects of intelligence on personality and political belief. Thus, no conspiratorial claims based on ethnic identity need to be given credence.*

> —"On the so-called 'Jewish Question'"

The problem was that having been nationally syndicated twice in my youth, first by *Chronicle Features* and then by *Universal Press Syndicate*, I knew perfectly well that some individuals of a certain persuasion, such as Ben Shapiro, just to provide a specific name, had been systematically promoted, presumably due to their ethnic identity, at the expense of more intelligent, more successful, and more popular colleagues. In my experience, Peterson's statement was flat-out wrong.

For example, when Ben Shapiro and I were both writing for World-NetDaily in the early 2000s, I was the third-most-read weekly columnist there, behind Pat Buchanan and Ann Coulter. Ben Shapiro, on the other hand, wasn't even in the top ten; if I recall correctly, his column readership numbers usually came in towards the bottom of the top twenty and averaged less than one-third of my own and one-fifth of Pat Buchanan's.

But while Ann Coulter and I were both signed to the elite *Universal Press Syndicate*, the less discriminating *Creators Syndicate* not only passed over most of the WND columnists who were observably more popular than Ben Shapiro, they told newspaper editors that they had to take Shapiro's column if those editors wanted to run columns by other, more popular columnists syndicated by *Creators* in their newspapers.

Now, there is nothing wrong with that. I certainly would have appreciated it if UPS had done the same for me and packaged my column with Ann's in a similar manner, but the white-shoe syndicate was above such unseemly high-pressure sales tactics. The point is, they were utilized and there is no question that my young colleague was the inexplicable beneficiary of them. Nor was that the only time I witnessed the very ethnic nepotism that Peterson denied.

What struck me even more than Peterson's false assertions was the vehemence with which he expressed his incorrect conclusions. To put it simply, the professor protested too much.

That was not the only problem with his statements. As a result of having done some research into declining national IQ averages in a book that I wrote back in 2015 with John Red Eagle, I not only knew that Jordan Peterson's claim of an average Jewish IQ advantage of 10-15 points over the white American population was false, I also knew the original basis for the claims of an average 115 Ashkenazi IQ and the weak scientific foundation upon which they rested. Even worse for Jordan Peterson, I immediately saw that he was statistically illiterate, given that his assertion necessarily implied that all the non-Ashkenazi Jews on the planet possess a lower average IQ than African-Americans.

Allow me to briefly explain: the population of Israel is 74.5 percent Jewish, of whom 47.5 percent are Ashkenazi Jews, the latter being 36 percent of the total population. Given the average reported Israeli IQ of 95 and the average reported Jordanian IQ of 84 serving as a proxy for Arab Israelis, an average 115 IQ for Ashkenazi Jews would necessarily indicate that all the other Jews on the planet have an average IQ of 84.2, which is slightly below the average reported African-American IQ of 85.

Does that sound right to you? If you wish to contemplate the issue in more detail, you can read the analysis in one of the appendices. And before you leap to the erroneous conclusion that my position is somehow anti-Semitic, please note that I am not the one claiming Sephardic and Mizrahi Jews have a reported average IQ more than one standard deviation *below* Europeans.

To top it all off, it was evident that Peterson did not realize that the original claim of very high Jewish IQ in the U.S.A. was based on a very small sample of elite Jewish elementary school children that was published in 1957 and was similar to another study of the era that reported *an average 119 IQ* for white Christian American children. As it happens, neither study was even remotely relevant to the average IQs of the relevant populations at the time, much less 62 years later, by the admission of Boris Levinson himself, the author of "The Intelligence of Applicants for Admission to Jewish Day Schools" published in *Jewish Social Studies*, Vol. 19, No. 3/4 (Jul.–Oct., 1957).

In short, the position Peterson was so vehemently defending was entirely built upon a foundation of intellectual sand. But when this was pointed out to him, in detail, by one of his readers who was familiar with my work, Peterson didn't even hesitate to double down. Even worse, he did so in an incredibly inept manner that raised serious questions about both his intellect and his integrity.

His attempt to defend his earlier errors proved to be disastrous. All that raising the cutoff for high IQ from one standard deviation to three standard deviations accomplished was to demonstrate his mathematical inadequacy. He was off by an order of magnitude with regards to the Jewish percentage of the 145+ IQ population in the United States, which is considerably closer to 3.7 percent rather than the 40.8 percent that Peterson has erroneously claimed.

That was the point at which I knew beyond any shadow of a doubt that Jordan Peterson was a charlatan, an intellectual fraud, and a wolf in sheep's clothing. An honest man, a genuine intellectual, simply does not make errors of that magnitude, then promptly proceed to make even bigger errors after being publicly called out and corrected.

That's what a con man who is attempting to salvage his con does. That's what someone who is dedicated to deceiving his audience does.

Now, there are no shortage of intellectual con men out there and I don't consider myself to be the Truth Police. Having confirmed for myself that Jordan Peterson was little more than a Canadian version of Deepak Chopra or L. Ron Hubbard, I was perfectly ready to return to completely ignoring him, but I was unable to do so thanks to his fans. Instead of accepting my critique, or even going over the various points in detail and attempting to rebut them, they attacked my intellect, my integrity, and my motivations. They accused me of jealousy, they accused me of envy, and they accused me of dishonesty, all in defense of a man who was observably lacking in any intellectual integrity at all! It was exceedingly bizarre, especially when I had done nothing more than point out a few of the obvious mistakes the man had made.

So, I decided to begin looking more deeply into this popular professor who was being so widely hailed as a formidable thinker, a thoughtful philosopher, a courageous defender of free speech, and a champion of young men. But almost immediately, I discovered that his reputation was at variance with his actions, as in the case of his deeply ironic decision to ban investigative journalist Faith Goldy from participating in an August 2017 event at Ryerson University called The Stifling of

Free Speech on University Campuses. The event was cancelled, and with Peterson's approval, Goldy was barred from participating in the rescheduled event.

When he was subsequently asked about his decision in public, Peterson responded with what I eventually came to recognize was his characteristic bafflegarble, the word-smog he habitually utilizes to conceal his actual meaning.

> *QUESTION: I understand that Faith Goldy was removed from the original August panel because of her podcast with the controversial Daily Stormer after Charlottesville.... This strategy appears to parallel the SJWs, who wish to deny platforms to conservative speakers. I want to understand why Faithy Goldy was removed from the event simply for associating with identitarians, and if each of the panelists agree with that decision.*

> *JORDAN PETERSON: That's an excellent question. So, the first thing I should say is that it's not like we're unaware of the irony. Number one. Ryerson cancelled a panel about the cancellation of panels about free speech. That's irony number one. And then irony number two was the panelists removed a speaker for arguably engaging in the act of free speech. Okay, we got that, believe me.*

> *All right, so why did we come to this decision? I sat down personally—the other people can say what they have to say—I sat down with my son and we went through Faith's interview. I know Faith, I don't believe that she is a reprehensible person. I think that Charlottesville was very shocking to her and I think that she put herself in a very difficult position. And I think some of that was brave, that she went down there to cover it.*

> *However, I listened very carefully to her podcast, the one that got her in trouble. And my sense was that she wasn't, she didn't, she was associating with people whose views she should have questioned. It*

was her journalistic, um, responsibility to question them. She had to ask at least one hard question. At least one. Three would have been better. You know, and I understand she had to toe a careful line. She was on the podcast, they had invited her on, it's much more difficult than you might think when you're facing people, even when you don't believe them, to be rude enough to challenge them, right? That's not so easy, especially if you're an agreeable person and she is a rather agreeable person.

But I believe she, she failed in her journalistic responsibility. And as a consequence of that, she became too hot a property for us. And not just for us. And, well, that was, that was the reason for the decision. That was, that was my reasoning.

Now, this was manifestly not the correct behavior of a highly principled man or even a reasonably honest one. Jordan Peterson did something he clearly knew to be wrong, he did something he clearly knew to be hypocritical, but instead of simply owning up to his obvious failure when called on it in public, he attempted to concoct a ridiculous *ex post facto* excuse to justify it. Again.

He had to know that he was going to have to face the question sooner or later. He even appears to have prepared for it, and yet this response was the best that he could manage. If you watch the video, you can even see that Jordan Peterson *has, he has,* a reliable tell that warns the viewer when he's about to say something that he knows is not true. He also betrays another tell that indicates when he is going to *very carefully* attempt to conceal the weakness of one of his assertions or conclusions.

Just watch for the repetitions and the adverbs. Once you learn to recognize them, you can identify when Jordan Peterson is trying to pull a fast one on his audience even when you don't know what he's talking about.

And the obvious question Peterson's response raises is this: according to what theory of human rights or journalism does one's own right to free speech rely upon one's correct performance of nonexistent journalistic responsibilities?

There is no such theory. It's a nonsensical assertion. It's classic Petersonian bafflegarble. But it requires a high level of mental focus to penetrate the fog of Peterson's word-salad and see what he is literally saying.

After twice seeing Peterson's shameless dishonesty in action, I decided that it was time to delve deeper into the man's actual work. Being a writer myself, I was aware that men express themselves differently in different media. Many eloquent speakers reveal themselves to be superficial thinkers in writing, and no few writers—myself included—are unable to express their genuinely profound thoughts in a facile manner in front of a microphone or a camera. Perhaps Peterson was much better in print than he was on video or on the Internet; after all, he was the bestselling author on the planet at the time.

So, I read his bestseller, *12 Rules for Life: An Antidote to Chaos*. I read his would-be magnum opus, *Maps of Meaning: The Architecture of Belief*. I even read his contribution to the UN Secretary General's High Level Panel on Sustainable Development of which he was a member, *Resilient People, Resilient Planet: A future worth choosing*.

And this book is the result of what I learned from reading the three published works of Jordan Peterson.

A word of warning. This book is necessarily more than a little esoteric. It references a number of works with which you may be unfamiliar, and draws obscure connections you may not immediately recognize or that you may be initially reluctant to acknowledge, especially if you are a Jordan Peterson fan.

But you can be sure of one thing. Unlike Jordan Peterson, I am not attempting to deceive, confuse, dazzle, or baffle you. Unlike Jordan Peterson, I am not attempting to change your perspective or your philosophy. Unlike Jordan Peterson, the logic I present is clear and straightforward. And unlike Jordan Peterson, I do not owe my allegiance to anything but the objective truth, as that concept has been defined in the dictionary and understood by Man since the beginning of time.

You need not take my word for any of this. Everything I am writing here is based on material evidence that you can obtain, examine, and analyze for yourself. So clear your mind, set aside your assumptions and preconceptions, and prepare yourself for a journey into the mind of one of the most shameless intellectual charlatans in the history of Man.

Chapter 1

Enter the Charlatan

Remember, falsehoods have consequences. That's what makes them false.

—Dr. Jordan Peterson

Jordan B. Peterson's self-help book, *12 Rules for Life: an Antidote to Chaos,* is a candidate to become Canada's best-selling book of all time. It is a number-one seller in North America and internationally. The author has 1.6 million YouTube subscribers, 904,000 Twitter followers, and a Patreon account believed to bring in over $100,000 per month in donations. He has been touring the United States in front of sold-out, adoring crowds buying tickets for as much as $400 a seat, and has recently signed with CAA, the agency to the Hollywood elite. He is the central figure of the *New York Times*-christened Intellectual Dark Web and is even rumored to have been selected to be television's next Oprah Winfrey.

The rise of the soft-spoken professor of psychology and his newfound prominence as an international thought leader and a father figure to hundreds of thousands of Millennials is a genuinely astonishing media phenomenon.

Most of his fans first encountered Peterson online, in one of his long, rambling videos. In addition to a large number of his classroom lectures, he also produces YouTube videos addressing his social and personal concerns as well as the interests of his massive online following. Others came across him by way of various media interviews, where he was seen to be addressing various social poisons, such as the newly discovered moral requirement to use ungendered pronouns or the idea that sexist payroll practices are the source of the alleged pay gap between men and women. Still others availed themselves of the various self-assessment and self-improvement services available on his website.

These things made him stand out amidst a culture under assault and in upheaval. The Western nations are adulterated and Western civilization is in decline. Young people attempting to enter the workforce struggle to find meaningful, reasonably-paid employment, and they are subject to relentless competition from more directions than ever before, from subsidized discount H1-B foreign workers to off-the-books illegals and affirmative action hires of dubious quality.

Not only that, but many of the jobs available appear to be more the makework consequence of globalized malinvestment than any genuinely productive business need. After all, what does a Social Media Specialist actually produce? Or, for that matter, a Project Manager or a Trust and Safety Council member? It isn't that these jobs, and hundreds of others like them can't be legitimate jobs under some circumstances. It is just that there is a sense that so many of the jobs available today are useless, unnecessary, underpaid and, ultimately, artificial. As frustrating as it may be to not have a job, it can in some ways be even more spiritually demoralizing to spend one's productive youth trapped in an occupation that is, by almost any measure, a pointless endeavor.

American society is in tatters, and from Millennials to Baby Boomers, Americans find themselves staring in dismay at the crumbling infrastructure, the rampant obesity, the shameless degeneracy, the increasing incivility, the political divide, and the breakdown of the family that surrounds them. They are seeking any port in a storm, yet finding nothing.

If the cultural bugaboo of youth in the 1950s was conformity, the hobgoblin of 2018 is individualism. Whereas iconoclastic wanderers like Jack Kerouac and the Beats sought to break the system, today's Millennials just want to find a system that is capable of working for them. The rise of identity politics and the chaotic fracturing of old alliances it involves can be attributed in part to this. People are desperate to belong, and since diversity has destroyed the old cultural bonds of community, school, church, and office, since divorce has broken the family, since the Boomers have finally shattered the system, individuals now have little choice but to find meaning and build bonds with others based on shared personal identities, however artificial they might be.

But group identity isn't quite as inclusive anymore as it used to be. In the past, straight white young women would naturally congregate within the traditional cultural system, either as stay-in-the-neighborhood moms, or possibly in the college system while working on an "Mrs." degree. Straight white young men would work alongside their kind, typically with some naturally occurring mentorship built in. There was no consciousness that such natural congregations could possibly be racist, any more than a transcurious asexual organism today would consider xirself to be sexist or normaphobic just for showing up at a campus LGBTQ meeting.

But as the social system became more diverse, it naturally continued to fracture. In the name of inclusiveness, immigration, and open borders, the system invited conflict and cultural war. And one of the most effective weapons in this uncivil war is to silence other groups and other identities before they have the chance to speak.

In other words, you aren't allowed to criticize the state of the culture today without being instantly stamped with one of the three unholy identities: racist, sexist, homophobic. If you say something—anything—that allows someone to mark you with one, two or even all three of those damnable offenses, then you will find yourself outed once and for all. Nothing you can say will ever be viewed outside the shadow of your single, right-wing, fanatical thought-crime.

And the Internet is forever.

Being a game designer, I often view reality through the lens of a computer game. Nick Bostrom's simulation hypothesis offers a modicum of intellectual justification for this perspective, but let's face it, it's a useful metaphor regardless. And there are times when the modern world feels like a live-action version of the game *Portal*, in which the environment is designed to kill you. However, unlike *Portal*, in the real world there is not a slowly disintegrating AI attempting to help you out. It's chaos out there, and you more or less have to find your way on your own.

Enter Jordan B. Peterson. The thoughtful, deeply-caring, avuncular professor from Canada offers a voice of apparent reason to young people, especially young men, who feel themselves to be lost and in desperate need of direction. He speaks in a careful and intelligent manner in his videos, and he dispenses simple, innocuous wisdom in an unobjectionable manner, asserting some basic truths, that, in an age of lies and mandatory self-deception, are received as if they were manna from Heaven by his listeners. The popularity of his ubiquitous video lectures fed the near-unprecedented demand for his second book, *12 Rules for Life*, which promises its readers a much-needed antidote to the chaos that he tells them fills their lives.

It is a remarkable thing that basic advice on how to behave as an adult, such as "stand up straight with your shoulders back" should be mistaken for a powerful, revolutionary response to societal chaos, but the truth is, there are many people who are so browbeaten by the ever-shifting rules of the ongoing cultural warfare that even simple childhood directives can be readily mistaken for the timeless wisdom of a true sage. And if a handful of simple, helpful truisms intended to help normal individuals survive an average day were the only message of *12 Rules for Life*, one could hardly object to it.

But that is not the case.

Contrary to what the average reader assumes, the twelve rules as written are not the primary message of Peterson's bestseller. In fact, the twelve rules, taken at face value, are not even relevant aspects of the real instructions hidden beneath them. Each rule is both a metaphor and a mask. And Jordan Peterson, like the homicidal GLaDOS of *Portal*, insists that he is only here to help.

Because encoded within the simple intellectual bait of the *12 Rules* is an insidious spiritual poison, and one of the purposes of this book is to help you identify and recognize it. Depending on your level of affinity for Jordan Peterson as a psychologist, a man, a therapist, and a mentor, this may be a difficult pill for you to swallow. But even if you are extremely skeptical of the thesis of this book, remember that even Jordan Peterson himself asks: "Why won't you take your damn pills?"

Reading Peterson can be a challenge, and many of his most ardent supporters have not read much, if any, of his published material, opting instead to rely on his vast video library of publicly available lectures, interviews and personal recordings. So, in case you have yet to approach his written work, it will be helpful to know that his so-called antidote to chaos is, like many antidotes, itself composed of poisons. There are three different spiritual poisons that feature prominently in the *12 Rules*: ignorance, narcissism, and mental illness.

Ignorance

Despite his intelligence and his unhesitating self-confidence in publicly addressing nearly any topic about which he is asked, Peterson's words frequently display a remarkable degree of ignorance of the subject upon which he is pontificating.

For example, when he elected to weigh in with his thoughts on the nomination and confirmation of Bret Kavanaugh to the United States Supreme Court, Peterson ignited a firestorm of indignation among his supporters when he suggested that Justice Kavanaugh step down from the court once his nomination was confirmed by the U.S. Senate following a bruising confirmation hearing that was dominated by nebulous accusations of criminal sexual assaults that supposedly took place more than three decades prior.

But one thing that escaped notice amidst the outrage was that in his subsequent non-apology, Peterson made it clear that he believed the position from which he thought Kavanaugh should step down was Chief Justice of the United States, not the open Associate Justice of the Supreme Court of the United States position to which he had actually been nominated.

> *It's not a good thing when there is general discomfort with the manner in which something as important as the naming of a new Chief Justice is undertaken. It doesn't bode well for the stability and peace of the state (and perhaps–perhaps–there is nothing more important to preserve than that).*

> —Jordan Peterson, "Notes on my Kavanaugh Tweet"

The fact that a Canadian was offering unsolicited advice to Americans on the composition of their highest legal institution was bad enough. The fact that he was doing so in obvious ignorance of the actual position involved was incredible, especially when one considers that The Honorable John G. Roberts, Jr. is still the Chief Justice of the United States, as he has been since 2005.

Despite the fact that the nomination and confirmation hearings had been in the news for the weeks, Peterson didn't even realize that Judge Kavanaugh was replacing the empty seat on the Supreme Court vacated by the retired Anthony Kennedy, who had served as an Associate Justice since 1988.

But Peterson's habit of opining in obvious ignorance is not limited to what he himself describes as the "dangerous platform" of Twitter and his own blog. He makes similarly egregious errors in the academic citations of his own books.

> *It was easier for people to be good at something when more of us lived in small, rural communities. Someone could be homecoming queen.*

Someone else could be spelling-bee champ, math whiz or basketball star. There were only one or two mechanics and a couple of teachers. In each of their domains, these local heroes had the opportunity to enjoy the serotonin-fuelled confidence of the victor. It may be for that reason that people who were born in small towns are statistically overrepresented among the eminent.

—12 Rules for Life

Peterson's citation for this statistical overrepresentation is from an article published by A.T. Poffenberger, "The Development of Men of Science," in the *Journal of Social Psychology* in 1930. This reliance on outdated, 87-year-old social science to retroactively extrapolate assumptions about the current overrepresentation of small-town among the eminent is extremely dubious from a scholastic perspective. But that is not even Peterson's worst intellectual crime in this case, because Peterson also incorrectly represents his source. In fact, in his article, Poffenberger states the *exact opposite* of the conclusion that Peterson ascribes to him:

The only comparison that can be made safely from this table is between two groups for a given size of birthplace, since we cannot tell what proportion of the population was living in the communities of various sizes. No significant differences appear which would enable us to conclude, e.g., that small towns are more likely than large to foster the production of eminent scientific men. *(Poffenberger, 1930)*

This is very far from the only example of Peterson's habitual ignorance on display throughout the *12 Rules*. First, since the facts don't support his argument, it is very convenient that he happened to reverse the original source's conclusions. Second, by relying on an obscure and irrelevant source, his ignorance of the source's actual conclusions are almost certain to go unnoticed by his readers who are attempting to follow his larger point and are unlikely to have access to scientific publications that are nearly a century out of date.

Given his customary ignorance, it probably will not surprise the reader to learn that Jordan Peterson began his public series of lectures on the Bible without bothering to read it first. A Lecturer in Philosophy at the University of St. Andrews, Alexander Douglas, notes that Peterson is similarly ignorant of one of his favorite topics, Marxism.

> *That he hasn't read any Marxist literature becomes obvious early on.... That he hasn't read any Marx is even more obvious.... Let's not pass by the fact that Peterson doesn't know when the Communist Manifesto was written. He says '1880 or 1890, whenever Marx wrote it.' Marx and Engels published it in 1848: a year that nobody remotely familiar with modern European history is likely to overlook. Marx was, of course, dead by 1883.*

—Alexander Douglas, "Review of Jordan Peterson's Stupid Lecture"

Narcissism

Jordan Peterson's books and lectures are punctuated with a large number of self-referential details, ostensibly in order to illustrate a point he is explicating, but Peterson's reliance upon his personal experiences is often improperly utilized. Time and time again, Peterson presents his own unique life experience as a definitive foundation for the common state of all mankind. There will often be times while reading *12 Rules for Life* that you will experience an amount of cognitive dissonance in response to Peterson's autobiographical assertions. Peterson will loftily claim something to be a universal truth for all people for all time, but his assertion will be something that is either not observably true in your own experience or something for which you can readily imagine various circumstances in which that claimed universal truth cannot possibly apply.

> *Beauty shames the ugly. Strength shames the weak. Death shames the living—and the Ideal shames us all. Thus we fear it, resent it—even hate it.*

—*12 Rules for Life*

> *I sloughed off a lot of my past. In a small town, everyone knows who you are. You drag your years behind you like a running dog with tin cans tied to its tail. You can't escape who you have been. Everything wasn't online then, and thank God for that, but it was stored equally indelibly in everyone's spoken and unspoken expectations and memory.*

—*12 Rules for Life*

> *Not all sacrifices are of equal quality. Furthermore, it often appears that sacrifices of apparently high quality are not rewarded with a better future—and it's not clear why. Why isn't God happy? What would have to change to make Him so? Those are difficult questions—and everyone asks them, all the time, even if they don't notice.*

—*12 Rules for Life*

> *I had a notion that confronting what terrified me—what turned my dreams against me—could help me withstand that terrible thing. This idea—granted me by the grace of God—allowed me to believe that I could find what I most wanted (if I could tolerate the truth; if I was willing to follow wherever it led me; if I was willing to devote my life to acting upon what I had discovered, whatever that might be, without reservation—knowing somehow that once started, an aborted attempt would destroy at least my self-respect, at most my sanity and desire to*

live). I believe now that everyone has this choice in front of them, even
when they do not know or refuse to admit it; that everyone makes this
choice, with every decision and action they take.

—*Maps of Meaning: The Architecture of Belief*

Peterson's penchant for autobiographical interpretation crops up repeatedly throughout both of his books. He viewed his experience of
growing up in a small town as being something to escape; a limiting
condition from which he sought to free himself. But Peterson's perspective is very far from universal. There are plenty of people who grow up
in small towns who never experience any of Peterson's oppressive sense
of hypervigilant oversight. In fact, there are many who view life in a
small town as one that is more friendly, safer and more reassuring than
the faceless anonymity of urban life. Peterson's personal perspective is
legitimate, but not the way in which he presents it as an unquestioned
universal example of the human condition. Peterson even admits as
much later when he writes "I thought that every person who moved
would have—and want—the same phoenix-like experience. But that
wasn't always the case."

Peterson frequently sets up his personal, egocentric experience as a
common universal event. It is "Autobiography as Everyman" and once
you know to look for it, its frequent appearances serve to tell the reader
considerably more about the author than about the human condition.
Perhaps this is why Peterson uses his ignorance of the facts of small-
town living less than twenty pages later, in the specious "eminent men"
argument. Peterson grew up in a small town. Peterson is now eminent,
perhaps the most famous living clinical psychologist today. His false
summary of Poffenberger's research serves as a sort of autobiographical
prophecy of Peterson's personal rise to eminence.

He justified this approach by an appeal to his intellectual mentor,
Carl Jung, in the same letter to his father quoted above.

Carl Jung has suggested that all personal problems are relevant to society, because we are all so much alike, and that any sufficiently profound solution to a personal problem may, if communicated, reduce the likelihood of that problem existing in anyone's experience in the future.

—Maps of Meaning: The Architecture of Belief

Peterson's narcissism means that his rules for life are literally his rules for his own life. Not yours and not mine. They are not a reliable guide towards a relevant philosophy for anyone who does not share a significant portion of the unique quirks, foibles, and flaws of a deeply damaged man.

Mental Illness

Peterson readily acknowledges that he, and a number of his family members, suffer from significant clinical depression and anxiety. Although he does not name a specific pathological diagnosis regarding his illness, one important clue is his admission to having had a tendency to habitually lie to himself and others at an unusually early age.

I soon came to realize that almost everything I said was untrue. I had motives for saying these things: I wanted to win arguments and gain status and impress people and get what I wanted. I was using language to bend and twist the world into delivering what I thought was necessary.

—12 Rules for Life

Peterson gradually grew more aware that his lying had become instinctual over time.

I learned to recognize when I was lying, in fact by noticing this sinking and division, and then inferring the presence of a lie. It often took me a long time to ferret out the deception. Sometimes I was using words for appearance. Sometimes I was trying to disguise my own true ignorance of the topic at hand. Sometimes I was using the words of others to avoid the responsibility of thinking for myself.

—12 Rules for Life

One is naturally inclined to wonder if Peterson still recognizes his own lies. For example, did he have that sinking feeling when he wrote his non-apology apology for conducting what he called "a thought experiment" in which he betrayed his own principles and sold out Supreme Court Justice Bret Kavanaugh by publicly encouraging Kavanaugh to resign after being confirmed by the U.S. Senate? Did he notice that he was lying? Was he disguising his own true ignorance? Or was he merely using the words of others to avoid responsibility?

Peterson exhibits an astonishing predilection for telling tall tales that don't even begin to pass muster. We're reliably informed by the man himself that he never, ever cheats on his diet, not even a little bit. Except, of course, for the famous time that he drank a glass of apple cider, now enshrined in Internet history as the notorious Cider of Doom.

It's readily apparent that Peterson has not succeeded in kicking his habit of habitual lying. In June 2018 he told Scott Oliver of *Vice*, "If I had my druthers I'd rather not be speaking politically at all," which flies directly in the face of his youthful campaign for the vice-presidency of Canada's socialist New Democratic Party at the age of 14, to say nothing of his musings concerning a possible run against Prime Minister Justin Trudeau only a month later, in July.

I won't be happy until I'm elected Prime Minister.

—Jordan Peterson, *Edmonton Journal*, March 14, 1977

What many Peterson fans fail to recognize is that his repeated ex-
hortations to tell the truth are no more indicative of Peterson being
inordinately truthful than Google's famous motto of "don't be evil"
means that Google is less inclined to commit evil actions than any other
giant, soulless corporation.

Just as "don't be evil" takes on a distinctly different meaning when
one envisions a wild-eyed, unshaven man stumbling through the night
with a knife in his hand muttering "don't be evil, don't be evil" to himself
as he eyes a pair of young women waiting at a nearby bus stop, "tell the
truth—or, at least, don't lie" takes on a very different meaning when it
is uttered by a narcissistic liar.

And remember, as I've already shown you, Peterson's rules are, first
and foremost, directed at himself. Do you need to remind yourself to
not lie on a regular basis? It is only the pathological liar who requires
such reminders.

Wikipedia informs us that "pathological lying is a stand-alone disorder, as well as a symptom of other disorders such as psychopathy and
antisocial, narcissistic, and histrionic personality disorders.... Sufferers
have also shown above average verbal skills as opposed to performance
abilities."

Is this starting to sound like anyone you know?

Mental illness runs in Jordan Peterson's family, which we are informed has suffered from depression for four generations. His daughter
Mikhaela has said that she was diagnosed with severe depression and
prescribed "a very high dose" of an SSRI called Cipralex from the age
of 12. Peterson himself stated that he takes two anti-depressants in a
2012 interview.

I did well on the serotonin reuptake inhibitor alone, but the addition
of the Wellbutrin definitely put in something that was missing. When
I first started to take it, which in some ways is a momentous decision,
especially for someone like me, because I pride myself in some ways on
having extremely tight control of my thoughts, for example. And even

when I was very depressed, and I've been VERY depressed, I've never had the cognitive portion of depression.... I have a lot of projects on the go, the equivalent, probably, of four full-time jobs.

—Jordan Peterson, *Depression: A Family Affair*

There is also an amount of mental illness in Jordan Peterson's social circle. His childhood friend and former roommate Chris spent more than a year living with Peterson and his family, during which time Peterson claims his evil-smelling friend only avoided murdering the entire family because Peterson happened to sense "the spirit of Cain had visited our house" at 4 AM and talked his friend down from what he describes as a "murderous rage."

Despite Peterson's expert ministrations, ten years later, at the age of 40, Chris committed suicide in the Canadian bush.

In that 2012 interview, Peterson declared that he would never stop taking anti-depressants, which, given his self-centered perspective, one tends to suspect is the foundation for the second of the 12 rules, Take Your Pills.

However, only six years later, Jordan Peterson publicly announced on the Joe Rogan show that he was no longer taking his medication due to the miraculous consequences of his ketogenic diet. He explained that this diet, in addition to curing his lifelong depression and anxiety, had also restored his energy, eliminated his gastric reflux, his snoring, his inability to get up in the mornings, his psoriasis, his gingivitis, the floaters in his right eye, the numbness of his legs, his gum disease, and his mood swings.

He is now, he declares, at his intellectual best. He's stronger and he can even swim better too!

Now, I am not a psychologist. I am not a psychiatrist either. I'm not even an aromatherapist or sandplay therapist. I consider Sigmund Freud to have been a fraud. I think psychotherapy is about as scientifically legitimate as astrology. I have no problem at all believing that antidepressant drugs will seriously mess with your mind and your body. I am not professionally competent to formally diagnose the sanity, or the lack thereof, of anyone.

But if you can't see that Jordan Peterson is a pathological nutcase with a Messiah complex and delusions of grandeur, you simply are not paying sufficiently close attention.

This isn't going to end well.

Chapter 2

Postulants of the 12-Rule Path

It is undignified to participate in the pitiful pageant of such colossally transparent intellectual fraud, standing around cheering 'well caught, sir!' at a man whose lectures are one long insult to his audience's intelligence.

—Alexander Douglas

One of the most remarkable things about Jordan Peterson is the stubbornly blind faith in him exhibited by so many of his followers. There is virtually nothing that can convince a true believer in Jordanetics that their Father Figure is a fraud, as they can effortlessly produce imaginative, incredible explanations, no matter how far-fetched, that they use to rationalize even the most indefensible behavior. It's rather like expressing one's doubts to a Hillary Clinton fan about the incredible success of her brief cattle-future-trading career, when, as the First Lady of Arkansas, she somehow managed to beat estimated odds of one in 31 trillion to make a profit of almost $100,000 in ten months.

In like manner, no matter how improbable the explanation, no matter how unlikely the excuse, the true Jordan Peterson fan will cling to it rather than face the observable facts about their intellectual hero. To say that they have drunk the Kool-Aid doesn't really do proper justice to the fervor of their faith.

In the six months following my inadvertent discovery of Jordan Peterson's chalatanry, I made a series of 17 YouTube videos discussing my various findings as I came across them, beginning with *The Problem with Jordan Peterson* on April 25th, 2018. With titles such as *The Madness of Jordan Peterson* and *Jordan Peterson Sells Out America*, it's not at all difficult to understand that more than a few Peterson fans were inclined to take umbrage.

And it wasn't just Jordan Peterson's fans who very much disliked the fact that I was turning a critical eye upon him. I was reliably informed that 80 percent of the members of a group that is primarily made up of my strongest and most long-term supporters were unhappy with what they saw as inexplicable attacks on a man who was on our side, what they felt was an unjustified betrayal of a fellow defender of tradition, Christianity, America, and the West.

Both sets of fans found the facts I was presenting very difficult to refute. But whereas my fans gave me a fair shake and waited for me to read Peterson's three published works, the cargo cultists resorted to an intriguingly wide variety of putative refutations, ranging from accusations of mental illness, involuntary celibacy, and professional envy to sexual attraction, personal obsession, and raw, unadulterated malevolence.

Following are a list of comments left on my YouTube channel, *Darkstream by Vox Day*, each in response to one of the 17 aforementioned videos. They are all reasonably representative of the positions being taken by the pro-Peterson commenters; I did not select any of the openly vulgar or more over-the-top examples because it is not my intention to pose as any sort of victim or appeal to the reader's sympathies, the comments are chiefly interesting for how they show how the fan fervor observably weakened as the video series continued over time.

You are standing on very shaky ground by boldly asserting that Peterson may be intentionally trying to deceive the public by using data that you say he is likely to know is incorrect or flawed. Peterson's evaluation of Jewish success due to a higher IQ is popular consensus based upon real data.... You seem to be jumping the gun with your opinion on Peterson. I would certainly enjoy watching you debate him. Your arrogance and ill constructed arguement of Peterson's use of questionable data to formulate his general observation reflects upon your ability to evaluate people and issues.

—hk, *DARKSTREAM: The Problem with Jordan Peterson*

You must demonstrate that Peterson's sources are the sources you claim. Moreover, if his sources have overstated the case (as you claim), the real error is in the sources, in which case your argument is not with Peterson but with those sources. You aren't arguing with Peterson. You are informing Peterson. With better data, Peterson's position may change. Or he may be using sources other than those you claim are so discredited.

—Christoper Ash, *DARKSTREAM: The Problem with Jordan Peterson*

You are clearly not efficient to understand the depth of Jordan. You look more like an autistic 13 year old.. old man that tries to get publicity points. That's why you are interested on Peterson. Isn't it? You just heard about Peterson few days ago and you were able to listen to his lectures? Probably not. You are too busy thinking how to get subscribers. Learn to be humble and recognize where you can move with your limited intellectual skill. What a pity.

—somchai shanabi, *DARKSTREAM: The Lunacy of Jordan Peterson*

And this fellow claims to have a gd read of JBP after watching his videos for 1 minute? Incredible intellectual dishonesty and desperation for attention is all i see here

—Ainomugisha Don, *DARKSTREAM: The Lunacy of Jordan Peterson*

Wow, Jordan Peterson is living in this guy's head, bigtime. Voxday needs to get out more, not that he has any chance of getting any.

—Drive Tone, *DARKSTREAM: The Lunacy of Jordan Peterson*

Your body language screams arrogant jealousy. You're a jealous hater.

—Matthew Joseph Ventresca, *DARKSTREAM: The Lunacy of Jordan Peterson*

You spoke of people thinking you were egotistical, they may have been right. Your whole speech is depressing, and you are unable and just plainly unwilling to say anything genuinely positive about him. You throw out certain things just so people think your being objective but these are not honest. The difference is that Jordan Peterson is honest and people follow him because of that—he is not trying to pull a fast one on anybody. We know he is trying to find truth and is passing those truths he has found. Evidence is him sticking his neck out when defending freedom of speech. He was unwilling to fold although many would have. That's why the things you say are not believable and honesty it is boring. Difficult to watch.

—Ramon Guzman, *DARKSTREAM: Jordan Peterson is Bait for the Broken*

Dude your like weird stalker obsessed with Peterson. It's obvious your the loon here that is ONLY JEALOUS that Peterson is a better man then you. I only say he's a better man then you because he doesn't ever go around bashing you. Your obviously crazy, move on.

—weirdotter930, *DARKSTREAM: Why Jordan Peterson Doesn't Take His Pills*

I think your using his name for fame and click bate. Because he is the new media focus. I'm just curious if you were posting all these anti videos prior to his being shot into the spotlight?

—Brooke Mac, *DARKSTREAM: Twelve Things I Learned From "12 Rules For Life"*

You sound like a crazy person. You're missing all the good that he's doing and are annoyed he is not as far to the right as you. JP never said he was a right-winger, conservative. He says he's a "classic British liberal". To me, you are so much more creepy than him.

—Nick Te, *DARKSTREAM: The Core Purpose of Jordan Peterson*

I am not convinced J.P. is as wholly evil as V.D. states. I cut people slack, that J.P is perhaps misguided and might come around. But, as this goes forward, and JP keeps escalating and ignoring, I am willing to admit Vox may be correct.

—MrWJMalan, *DARKSTREAM: Jordan Peterson is an "anti-Semitic dog-whistler"*

At least Peterson respected his audience enough to stop smoking the pipe on days he puts out content. You could learn something there.

—Adam McCubbin, *DARKSTREAM: Jordan Peterson is a Globalist Shill*

It's ironic how Vox fits the "seven signs" himself.

—trollolol234, *DARKSTREAM: Seven Signs of an Intellectual Charlatan*

Have you read Peterson's books or looked at the 300+ hours of his college lectures on YouTube? He's a clinical psychologist focused in part on the men's rights, freeing the mind, beating depression, how to quit procrastination etc etc with solution based models that actually work. Peterson would run circles around you in a debate of ideas.

—t8888, *DARKSTREAM: An Apology to Jordan Peterson*

There are many reasons to avoid someone (that is, to 'block' or 'deplatform'). Maybe Jordan Peterson just found Faith Goldy annoying, or unhelpful to the discussion. Maybe it didn't have anything to do with her 'opinions' at all.

—Frank Norris, *DARKSTREAM: Jordan Peterson is a Free Speech Fake*

This is intellectual hubris at it's finest. You first so called "answer" was predicted on the premise that objective truth exists. There is no objective truth. Maybe an objective reality a material reality. That reality exists independent on an observer. The observer actually gives that reality meaning and conceptualizes it. What reality would there be without consciousness? This whole idea of objective truth distorts the picture of reality into a conceptual average. Which displaces individuality and turns us into units from a mass formation. Some study in ontology or phenomenology may help to actually understand.

—Man Is Not his Own Master, *DARKSTREAM: 7 Answers to Jordan Peterson's Questions*

Vox is jealous and pathetic.

—Tzimtzum Alef, *DARKSTREAM: An Alt-Right response to Jordan Peterson*

Oh no! People are getting their lives together and becoming productive members of society! Oh the horror!

—Geoffrey McCorbin, *DARKSTREAM: Gateways or Gatekeepers*

Pathetic attempt to smear Dr. Peterson. Sure he is a bit old school but at least he is honest. You sir are not honest and you know it! Your jealousy is showing. How about you go accomplish something.

—w reed, *VOXIVERSITY: The Madness of Jordan Peterson*

7 minutes in and I can't continue. Was hoping for some MATURE criticism i.e, not continuously showing tiny clips of Peterson with his head down as if he is constantly overwhelmed or depressed or something. Taking that clip from the notorious Kathy Newman interview where even a squirrel can see she got annihilated, 'so you're saying we should organise our societies along the lines of lobsters' yeah don't show the next part where he puts his case for saying that in context, God forbid. Or putting that stupid voice editing on certain clips of his lectures to make it seem that he's not all there. If you have a point, make it. No need to attack and be a child about it. I encourage criticism, that's why I'm here, but I really can't take you seriously. I think those comments about you, Vox, are quite right. If you weren't jealous or petty you had your chance to prove that you're not with this video. Unfortunately you proved those comments right.

—Stephen Johnson, *DARKSTREAM: The Madness of Jordan Peterson*

Peterson fans being losers isn't an argument. Not everyone has the privilege of coming from a well adjusted two parent households. He has measurably helped thousands be better people. This is unequivocally a good thing.

—Brewmaster Monk, *DARKSTREAM: The Cultists Strike Back*

You say you're not jealous of Peterson, but somehow I suspect you are, whether consciously or not. The whole 'St. Jordan Peterson' thing raises those suspicions. He never pitched himself as a saint. If yourself or others began to picture him like that and have now become disappointed that he's merely human, that's your own failing. He is, however in my opinion a great man doing his best to steer humanity in a positive direction as we all should.

—Stan Cooper, *DARKSTREAM: The Miracles of St. Jordan Peterson*

Some disagreement: Peterson has only been able to survive and gain tenure at a place like University of Toronto by being a certain way, including his weak ideas on theology and religion, and his very very careful thought before he speaks—a habit I should have learned when I was young. He's the best modern Academia can produce in most

*universities in Canada and quite a few in the US. To be honest if he
even just said "Yes I believe there's a God" he'd be nailed. ONLY a guy
like him could even SURVIVE in that place. This is not an excuse. It's
an observation. Overall he's done huge good for many young men who
had not found anyone better–and the number of better men available
that these young men can easily find and connect with are sadly few in
number. He got a lot of guys off on the right direction–a lot of fatherless
men who never HAD anyone to tell them the basics of cleaning your
room, standing up straight, why respectfulness and truthfulness are
good, etc. Even if he is intellectually a vacillator.*

—Red Pill Religion, *DARKSTREAM: Jordan Peterson stars as
Wormtongue!*

But the increasingly moderate nature of the comments as the series
went on was not the only indication that the faith of Peterson's followers
was proving to be less than unshakeable in the face of reason and
revelation. Because YouTube allows viewers to indicate their approval
or disapproval of a video, it is possible to track the general trend of the
ratio of approval/disapproval over time.

The first video I recorded, a Darkstream entitled *The Problem with
Jordan Peterson*, has had over 13,750 views, only a fraction of the
number that a Jordan Peterson or Stefan Molyneux video receives, and
met with a fairly favorable response due to the substantial case presented
in it. The 492 Likes outnumbered the 192 Dislikes, resulting in a 3.08x
ratio on YouTube.

The second video on the subject, *The Lunacy of Jordan Peterson*,
was less well-received, possibly because more Jordan Peterson fans had
become aware of the Darkstreams, or perhaps due to the more stringent
nature of the accusations I was beginning to make. The approval ratio
dropped to 1.95x, but as I continued to investigate Peterson and his
work, the viewers became increasingly confident in the case I was presenting to them. Eventually, the Like/Dislike ratio rose as high as 15x

for a video that addressed the question of whether the two Intellectual
Dark Web members, Jordan Peterson and Ben Shapiro, were acting as
gateways or gatekeepers for the ideological Right.

Below is a list of all 17 Darkstreams, plus one Voxiversity video, and
the various approval ratios for each. The higher the number, the greater
the approval by the viewers.

03.08 The Problem with Jordan Peterson

01.95 The Lunacy of Jordan Peterson

03.78 Jordan Peterson is Bait for the Broken

02.62 Why Jordan Peterson Doesn't Take His Pills

06.66 Twelve Things I Learned From "12 Rules For Life"

05.90 The Core Purpose of Jordan Peterson

11.78 Jordan Peterson is a Globalist Shill

08.33 Seven Signs of an Intellectual Charlatan

03.96 An Apology to Jordan Peterson

19.31 Jordan Peterson is a Free Speech Fake

10.37 7 Answers to Jordan Peterson's Questions

11.39 An Alt-Right response to Jordan Peterson

15.14 Gateways or Gatekeepers?

09.97 The Cultists Strike Back

00.88 VOXIVERSITY: The Madness of Jordan Peterson

06.78 The Madness of Jordan Peterson

03.38 The Miracles of St. Jordan Peterson

13.76 Jordan Peterson stars as Wormtongue!

You will probably note that the approval ratio for the Voxiversity
video is considerably lower than for the other videos. For more on that,

read the next chapter. But it is interesting to note that the Darkstream that announced this book, *A Journey Into the Mind of Humanity's Greatest Thinker*, presently has a 35.12 Like/Dislike ratio.

The truth is winning.

Chapter 3

The Video Indictment

I'm a media whore, you know.

—Dr. Jordan Peterson

Unlike the aforementioned Darkstreams, which are simply extemporaneous streamed videos where I talk live to whoever happens to tune in, Voxiversity videos are professionally produced lectures that go deeper into a subject and tend to strike a little harder due to the way the producer effectively utilizes music and graphics to increase the emotional impact of the rhetoric. The production team tries to produce two Voxiversity videos a month, on a wide variety of subjects, including free trade, child abuse, Christianity, and the socio-sexual hierarchy.

At the request of the subscribers, we produced a video collecting what we had learned about Jordan Peterson over the previous four months and released it. The Voxiversity video, entitled *The Madness of Jordan Peterson*, is extremely hard-hitting and utilizes footage of Peterson at his contemptible worst, rambling and incoherent, emotionally incontinent, and intellectually inconsistent.

At the time of this writing, it presently has just over 33,000 views, less than one-tenth the number of the Q&A video on Peterson's YouTube channel posted around the same time. The transcript follows:

DAVE RUBIN: We are live with a man who I think at this point needs no introduction.

VOICEOVER: The most influential public intellectual in the Western world, one of the world's most controversial thinkers.

JORDAN PETERSON: Hi.

VOICEOVER: Jordan Peterson! Professor Jordan Peterson. Jordan Peterson!

VICE NEWS TONIGHT: Peterson gained national notoriety when he spoke out about a federal bill on gender expression.

JORDAN PETERSON: I am NOT going to be a mouthpiece for language that I detest and that's that.

FAIRFAX MEDIA: His new self-help book, *12 Rules for Life*, is already a best-seller. Hundreds of thousands subscribe to his online lectures, his speeches regularly attract protests and his new speaking tour is selling out.

WOMAN: Feels like a movement and I'm excited to be a part of it.

RAN DOSIS, ARTIST: Dr. Peterson has changed my life. He has reminded me that I should first and foremost, should clean my room.

VOICEOVER: Tell us about the lobsters.

JORDAN PETERSON: Ha! Well, that's quite a segue! I think the whole group identity thing is seriously pathological.

CATHY NEWMAN: Let's get this straight. You're saying that we should organize our societies along the lines of the lobsters?

JORDAN PETERSON: The way that you deal with this is to put yourself together.

ALEX JONES: We don't need to be taught how to wipe our ass by Jordan Peterson!

VOX DAY: What good is a clean room in Rome going to do when Alaric the Goth is sacking your city?

JORDAN PETERSON: The group identities emerge only when necessary.

VOX DAY: They're trying to come up with a way to keep the right on the reservation and that's what Jordan Peterson is doing in the world of philosophy which I call Jordanetics. It is ultimately anti-Christian, it's poisonous, and it's riddled from start to finish with mental illness.

JORDAN PETERSON: (cries)

VOX DAY: This guy is the Crazy Christ! I mean, he has a Messiah Complex. He actually wrote to his father and said:

JORDAN PETERSON: I think I've discovered something that no one else has any idea about.

VOX DAY: It's clear that we're not dealing with somebody who is mentally well.

JORDAN PETERSON: It was literally driving me crazy. Dreaming extremely violent dreams. What shall I do with my newfound Pen of Light? I waited for a reply, and almost immediately an answer revealed itself: write down the words you want inscribed on your soul.

MUSIC: (the Hallelujah Chorus)

JORDAN PETERSON: I'm a media whore, you know.

VOX DAY: The Madness of Jordan Peterson

VOX DAY: Although I had heard about a Canadian academic who became an unexpected hero to American conservatives through his YouTube videos and a best-selling self-help book I did not pay Jordan Peterson any notice until it was brought to my attention that he was repeating exaggerated and long disproven claims about the intelligence of a minority group.

JORDAN PETERSON: The average Ashkenazi IQ is somewhere between 110 and 115, which is about one standard deviation above the population average.

VOX DAY: While anyone can be misled by unreliable sources, what made me suspicious of his intellectual integrity was the way that he immediately doubled down and resorted to name-calling and disingenuous rhetoric when called out for his error by his better-informed readers. The way in which I was energetically denounced by his fans and accused of everything from jealousy to mental retardation for the heinous crime of publicly correcting him only made me more dubious about the man. It didn't take very long to discover that the man was something very very different than the public figure whom conservatives were praising so highly.

GREG QUEEN'S JOURNAL: What do you think of the things that people, and I'm especially thinking of your opponents, get wrong about you?

JORDAN PETERSON: Their basic proposition is that, you know, first of all, that I'm a right winger of some sort, and that's just not the case.

VOX DAY: Virtually nothing that is believed to be true about Jordan Peterson is actually true. Jordan Peterson is not a Christian. Jordan Peterson is not a conservative. Jordan Peterson is not a defender of Western civilization or Western culture. Jordan Peterson is not post-ideological. Jordan Peterson is not a hero. Jordan Peterson is not a right-winger of any sort. Jordan Peterson is not a prophet. Jordan Peterson's thoughts are not too advanced for ordinary people to follow. And most importantly, most of the time, Jordan Peterson simply does not know what he's talking about.

JORDAN PETERSON: What the hell do I know about it? Ha ha ha ha ha ha!

VOX DAY: Nirmal Dass, a Canadian author and PhD who specializes in translating ancient languages, observes that Jordan Peterson is poorly educated and lacks a basic knowledge of religion, history, theology, philosophy, science, and logic. He writes: "He misconstrues the Logos and blasphemes his way through the Old Testament and the Gospel. As for history, just one example suffices: No, Jesus is not a version of the Egyptian god Osiris. This nonsense comes from Gerald Massey, a 19th century crackpot who faked evidence to make such claims."

JORDAN PETERSON: Keep talking, bucko. Pretty soon I'm going to have you right where I want you.

VOX DAY: This comprehensive charge of general ignorance may sound difficult to believe.

JORDAN PETERSON: And I've always felt like a complete idiot.

JORDAN PETERSON: So there, there now. I've got my Kwakwaka'wakw.

VOX DAY: But remember Jordan Peterson admitted that he had never even read through the entire Bible before he began delivering his series of lectures on it.

JORDAN PETERSON: Jesus, you know, what the hell did I do?

VOX DAY: The readily observable fact is that very few Jordan Peterson fans have ever taken any trouble to actually read what he has written. Unlike most of his fans I've read the *12 Rules*, *Maps of Meaning*, and the United Nations Secretary General's high-level panel on global sustainability, *Resilient People, Resilient Planet: A Future Worth Choosing*, and I can attest that the charge of comprehensive ignorance is an accurate one.

VOX DAY: For example, throughout the entire five hundred and sixty four pages of *Maps of Meaning* there are precisely zero direct references to such minor intellectual figures as Aristotle, Socrates, Epictetus, Augustine, Marcus Aurelius, and Thomas Aquinas. By way of example, no man even remotely familiar with the Greek and Roman skeptics could possibly have produced such an incredibly ignorant statement as this:

JORDAN PETERSON: Prior to the time of Descartes, Bacon and Newton, Man lived in an animated spiritual world saturated with meaning imbued with moral purpose but now we think empirically and the spirits that once inhabited the universe have vanished.

VOX DAY: The clue is right there in the most famous skeptic's name. Sextus Empiricus.

JORDAN PETERSON: I'm very, very, very careful with my words.

VOX DAY: Jordan Peterson's customary approach to a subject is to take simple straightforward concepts and redefine them in order to transform their core meanings to suit whatever he is saying at the moment. Even worse he assigns multiple meanings and contradictory definitions to those concepts, making it literally impossible to know with any degree of confidence what he's actually saying. He does this in order to allow the listener to assign his own meaning to Peterson words.

VOX DAY: It's a psychological technique that can be described as pre-emptive mirroring, as Peterson's rambling incoherence permits the listener to hear what he is seeking to hear and feel that his preconceived views are substantiated by the authority of Peterson's presumed wisdom. Peterson is purposefully saying nothing in order to leave a hole of meaning that the listener will dutifully provide and credit to him. This is why different Peterson fans will almost invariably disagree about what he has said.

VOX DAY: Peterson says, "When I lecture I'm not saying what I believe to be the case but thinking on my feet trying to extend and clarify my knowledge while also communicating." To the extent that there is any actual content of Peterson's lectures they are narcissistic monologues aimed primarily at himself. This is why those who have read Peterson's books tend to have a much lower opinion of him than those who attend his lectures and watch his videos. His technique of pre-emptive mirroring does not work when one can so easily see the contradictions and incoherencies littering each and every page, but when he's on stage, if you react poorly to one of Peterson's positions you have only but to wait a little while and he will produce another one you will find more to your liking.

JORDAN PETERSON: Clean up your room!

VOX DAY: Peterson's incoherent and self-contradictory philosophy can best be described as Clintonian as he repeatedly redefines everything from Christianity to God and the very concept of truth itself. Just listen to these absurd, nonsensical definitions he puts forward when asked what he means by God.

JORDAN PETERSON: God is the mode of being you value the most. The spirit that is trying to elevate being. It makes everything come together. The truthful speech that rectifies pathological hierarchies. How we imagine and collectively represent the existence and action. Consciousness across time. The selection mechanism which judges which men are worthy.

VOX DAY: Collectively, these statements can clearly be seen to be pure bafflegrab. String them together and you'll see that they're entirely nonsense. A truthful speech is a selection mechanism that rectifies pathological hierarchies which is how we imagine the existence of consciousness trying to elevate being? That's nonsense.

JORDAN PETERSON: I think that's silly. I really do.

VOX DAY: And it leads to the obvious question: what makes speech truthful? If Peterson is to be believed, truth is that which serves life in a Darwinian manner.

JORDAN PETERSON: Like the fundamental axiom that I'm playing with is something that was basically expressed by Nietzsche and it's a definition of truth. And so I would say if it doesn't serve life it's not true.

VOX DAY: Or to put it more bluntly and clearly, the truth, the Darwinian pragmatic truth to be specific, is anything you believe that happens to increase your odds of survival. This, you will note, is a concept that directly contradicts the concept of truth as the dictionary and pretty much everyone else in the history of the planet has ever understood it.

JORDAN PETERSON: Okay, that makes sense. EXCEPT! I would say that God is dead and human beings are like a cancer on the planet.

VOX DAY: Thanks to this perverted redefinition of truth Peterson even concludes that facts are not necessarily true.

JORDAN PETERSON: Then I would say that I don't think that facts are necessarily true.

VOX DAY: But Peterson doesn't just play philosophically fast and loose when it comes to facts, figures, and definitions. He can't even answer a straightforward yes-or-no question honestly.

TIMOTHY LOTT: Do you believe that Jesus rose again from the dead?

JORDAN PETERSON: (thinks)

TIMOTHY LOTT: Literally.

JORDAN PETERSION: I find I cannot answer that question, and the reason is, because, okay let me think about it for a minute see if I can come up with a reasonable answer to that. Well, the first answer would be, it depends on what you mean by Jesus.

TIMOTHY LOTT: A historical human being that existed.

JORDAN PETERSON: In a body?

TIMOTHY LOTT: In a body.

JORDAN PETERSON: In a body. Do you believe that or do you not believe it? You know, it's not, it's... I don't know.

VOX DAY: Now come on! Is this really the first time that Peterson has ever considered that question? And yet he did manage to answer a related question a little bit more directly. Do you go to church?

JORDAN PETERSON: No. In my experience, the ministers are too frequently lying. I can't stand to hear them say words they don't believe.

VOX DAY: But how could a man who doesn't even know what he believes possibly know what others truly believe? How can he know they are lying about Jesus when that would entirely depend upon what they mean by Jesus, and how can a man who claims that facts are not necessarily true possibly claim that anyone else is lying?

VOX DAY: Now we've recently seen Peterson and public figures on the Left who have been elevated and promoted as an acceptable opposition by the mainstream media; the most notorious example being the *New York Times's* proclamation of the intellectual dark web that includes Jordan Peterson, Ben Shapiro, and Sam Harris, among others, and the reason that they've been elevated is because their whole job is to prevent young men from moving towards nationalism and Christianity in their ongoing rejection of the neo-liberal world order.

JORDAN PETERSON: That's why I'm talking to... I'm trying to call them forth as individuals out of the chaos that they're ensconced in.

VOX DAY: If you pay attention, you notice that none of these members of the approved opposition are Christians, and more importantly, everything you see come out of their mouths is anti-nationalist.

BEN SHAPIRO: A person who is living abroad in Japan could be more of an American than a person who's born in Ohio.

VOX DAY: Now, it's not always directly anti-nationalist and Jordan Peterson is much more clever than Ben Shapiro in this regard.

JORDAN PETERSON: The distance between the typical citizen and the bureaucracy that runs the entire structure has got so great that it's an element of destabilization in and of itself, and so people revert back to, say, nationalistic identities because it's something that they can relate to.

VOX DAY: What Peterson does is to criticize globalist institutions like the European Union and the United Nations because he thinks that they are moving too far, too fast, for the public to accept.

JORDAN PETERSON: Because we're not built for static utopia, we're built for a dynamic situation.

VOX DAY: But the reality is, his long term objectives are almost identical to the long term goals of George Soros and other globalists. That may sound improbable but in a recent interview with George Soros, the great financier of Antifa and global society rather improbably insisted that he is non-ideological. Jordan Peterson also claims to be non ideological despite his globalism, his employment by the United Nations, and his history as a socialist activist.

VOX DAY: In that same interview, George Soros said that his main concern was that the Left has become too extreme, which happens to be precisely the same concern that was revealed by Peterson what was billed as a debate on political correctness with Stephen Fry, Michael Dyson, and Michelle Goldberg.

JORDAN PETERSON: Political correctness: it's about the left going too far, and I think it's gone too far in many ways. And I'd like to figure out exactly how, and win so the reasonable left could make its ascendance again and we could quit all this nonsense.

VOX DAY: Jordan Peterson is trying to fix globalism. He's actively seeking to destroy your nation and your faith because he believes it's necessary in order to save the world. So in conclusion, I'll ask you this. For what shall it profit a man if he shall clean his room and lose his own soul?

The reaction of the Jordan Peterson fans to this withering, openly contemptuous unmasking of their hero was emotional distress with occasional forays into full-blown derangement. Here are a few responses that are representative of the 866 comments that were left on the YouTube video alone.

Jordan Peterson crazy? If I recall the family of Jesus said that about him at one point and went to get him. Mr Peterson is eccentric yes. But nothing worthy of this level of axe grinding. I researched the author of this video and I do suspect motives that I would not call Christian. The best thing about JP is getting people to think and form a coherent opinion. He is spot on resisting regulated speech laws. That does not mean I embrace his dialogue about lobsters. I take the good with the bad which many of us do today with Donald Trump.**

—Daniel Wessel, *VOXIVERSITY: The Madness of Jordan Peterson*

I don't care if you agree with him or not, for a man who never tries to attack someone's character, the editing and insulting takes down any real argument you have, regardless of religion being flat out baseless and without logic, when it comes to god isn't it the Christian way to let people believe in what they believe in their own way, or do you need to be as authoritarian as possible, and before you call me some leftist soy boy or cuckservative I'm a centrist, with a long history of reading about the idea of religion and god, and while I don't agree with everything Peterson says, he conducts himself with remarkable civility, try to learn about that.

—Tigerairlines, VOXIVERSITY: The Madness of Jordan Peterson

You've kind of glossed over his points and glittered them with quick pics of lobsters and a kid saying he'll clean his room. When in reality if you read the book, his uses of simple ideas to build on larger ones is pretty novel. When you're being that willfully obtuse, I can't respect your viewpoint. Whether you agree with him or not he's no fraud. You can disagree, but to bash a guy for holding different views than you is just kind of being a catty baby.

—Charms434, VOXIVERSITY: The Madness of Jordan Peterson

Poorly done video. You've failed to make any real dent into his character and intellect. In short you've shown your ignorance and obsession with God.

—Fank234, VOXIVERSITY: The Madness of Jordan Peterson

This is a very cringeworthy video. The editing is quite shocking, and totally distracts from any points you choose to make. Yes, some of his many fans are deluded and seeking leadership, and he is frequently obscure, however, he has more than proved himself worthy of his current position. It is simply not true to say his elevation has been born through adulation. He has been made in opposition to great criticism. A lesser person, you for instance, would have crumpled after a few months. He has balls. That's the first thing. Next, for his simple referencing of Solzenhitsyn, Frankl and Dostoevsky to a new generation he is to be greatly commended. No, Aristotle and other greats are not mentioned, so fucking what? He was not writing a treatise on Western thought, just a string of ideas. Finally, his central message is very simple, namely life is hard if you live it and suffering is always present. This is a core idea of Christianity and Buddhism and exists because it is true. This is liberating to many who have been told that perfection is a goal, happiness is achievable and self worth is defined by how many bucket list items you tick off. He has simply reinstated a core experience of life and articulated in a way that people can understand. It has transformed people's lives, whether you find him phoney or not. No one has managed to do this for about 70 years, no one. Therapists, gurus, and even traditions religion has failed in this, and it took an obscure professor from Canada to do this.

You have been accused of jealously, and that accusation stands. The hatchet job here is quite pathetic, since you just pick away at trivia. I have stated clear arguments above, which demonstrate very simply that he has done a good thing, by introducing just a few core ideas (complexity of life, suffering, personal responsibility and the importance of the individual to the West). To criticise this is pure madness, and articulate as you are, your words are completely hollow. I suggest, without respect, you shut the fuck up, or actually comment on the positive contributions of this man over the last three years. I will now watch your channel and comment increasingly if I deem it fit. Some may read my thoughts. Some of us are sick of opinionated little clever shits, who do fuck all in the real world while assuming some sort of superiority in the digital. Ultimately it has no meaning. Peterson has let it all hang out, he has demonstrated integrity and seeks the good. He is not perfect, will be ephemeral, and will be followed by some sheep. However, give the man his due. You are jealous, and it is a very unpleasant character trait. I gained nothing from this video, accept the urge to come around your house and smash your fucking PC up. Now be a good chap, go and have a wank and take your hot chocolate.

—Largesse1000, *VOXIVERSITY: The Madness of Jordan Peterson*

Let me guess, your actually just upset he doesn't believe in your dogmatic Christian beliefs? Therefore, he's deserving of whatever pseudo-intellectual smear you can throw his way. You claim "Most of his fans haven't even read his stuff, but I have." Also, you're bitterness and snarky undertone in your passive aggressive rhetoric shines light on the fact that your simply offended he has strong arguments which threaten your own. You can disagree with Peterson without vilifying him. However, your video is a reflection of your inability to recognize this fact as well as a manifestation of your insecurity of your own beliefs. In other words, your simply not as intelligent as you seem to think you are.

—TheHarperbow, *VOXIVERSITY: The Madness of Jordan Peterson*

I understand Peterson's ideas quite well. I understand his conception of God/divinity and truth. I think the Jungian approach, which, at least partially, describes his metaphysics is extremely coherent and needs to be contended with by serious thinkers. This video is simplistic, disingenuous and is high on rhetoric. It takes Petersons output out of context. Chooses a few low hanging fruit and puts all its energies into discrediting Peterson. It's pulp. It's uses ad hominem tactics (a bankrupt tactic of the left).Many ideas JP has aren't from the man himself, they're based on deep wells of truth which we don't understand very well now. It's easy to get him and his ideas all wrong. The truth *is all this JP aversion is pure politics, and from the far left that means the truth is irrelevant, it's all about using any trick in the book to win the day. For a student of ideas, it's just boring.*

—jonathan spencer, *VOXIVERSITY: The Madness of Jordan Peterson*

This video is mostly false statements. Not tiny incorrect statements, but false statements that are 180 degrees off. I don't know what could be worse, the fact that someone did this video in good faith, but had an IQ that was so low they completely mis-characterized everything out of sheer stupidity, or that they were malicious enough to put this together as a hit piece to target the most brilliant man many of us have had the pleasure to listen to. Either way, shame on you, this is garbage!

—Greg Gustin, *VOXIVERSITY: The Madness of Jordan Peterson*

I think you have a wall of ignorance to pass. I think you're too smart for you're own good. If I could, I'd suggest getting much deeper into the study of 'intelligence capacity', and 'evolutionary psychology'. I think some of the concepts might open your mind.

Jordan isn't a god among men, nor a prophet of some form. He never claims to be. What he claims to be, is someone who is attempting to progress humanity altruistically. Now whilst you might have a problem yourself coming to grips the fact in purity that multiple forms of ultimate realities are reprovingly correct. Quantum Physics. 'Historical' Jesus. Sub-Consciousness. Undoubtedly, you don't have to see him as a god, to see how hard he works to actually create progress. He is one of the most widely known names right now, because he worked for it, he spent time educating himself, challenging and conditioning

*himself, and then marketing himself. To be ignorant of that, is to be
ignorant of one of the greatest attempts to progress humanity, whether
wrong or not, how about you help, instead of create tension, and
ignorance for others? You're obviously smart enough to understand the
concept, that a YouTube video will inspire some to think something
out of trust.*

*You are very well educated, and versed in philosophy and rhetoric, that
is obvious. Though I'd like to ask you to step out of that mindset before
making such large accusations against someone whom is just trying to
make the world better. If you really care, reach out to him, have a
discussion. Help progress this world together.*

*Let me tell you though, as much as it is an opinion. Watching such
intelligent people attack each other is becoming more disgusting to
watch. Speak to each other, work for the progress of humanity. Stop
doubting, and criticizing one another, then wondering why the world
is progressing in such a slow manner. Every body has to talk about
someone else's ignorance. Get involved in the larger picture, not your
own picture.*

—Fair Discussion, *VOXIVERSITY: The Madness of
Jordan Peterson*

*Now I'm a fan of Peterson, but I do take his talks with a grain of salt.
You do have a point about his avoidance of giving a direct answer.
But, what people that reject him don't appreciate, is the message he is
bringing forth that will help stabilise this increasingly polarising world
we're in. Between the left and right, religious and non religious, and
the Us vs Them mentality that's propagating in every sphere basically.
I would suggest to actually listen to the IDW, the recently available
Sam Harris and Jordan Peterson talk in Vancouver is a good start.*

What they're trying to do is build a bridge between the opposing poles of society.

—reslan kain, *VOXIVERSITY: The Madness of Jordan Peterson*

Its interesting how the Leftists feel so deeply compelled to discredit JP simply because they feel threatened when he intellectually refutes leftist ideology without the ability for them to respond with any meaningful or sensible response, The fact many leftists are left questioning their own beliefs or what they've been told all their life must be an extremely painful experience to bear. Some move back to a more traditional left position, other continue to attempt to debunk JP through countless failed interviews or silly uploads like this which actually enforce the positive message of JP.

—gravelsanga, *VOXIVERSITY: The Madness of Jordan Peterson*

This video does a poor job of challenging Peterson's weaker points and is mostly an Ad Hominem filled Smear Piece intended for people who lack critical thinking skills and seek to confirm rather than challenge their beliefs. Its very clear what you are trying to do here Vox, you cannot refute Jordan Peterson's arguments directly so you are resorting to mis-characterizations, straw man arguments, and repeatedly taking him out of context. Unfortunately for you this is a complete failure of a propaganda hit-piece and a prime example of how to ruin your reputation.

—BlizZinski, *VOXIVERSITY: The Madness of Jordan Peterson*

Love Jordan. He is a seeker and speaker of truth, and he tells you what his definition of truth is. His concept of truth is not the mundane dictionary definition and he tells you such. However you misrepresent his concept of truth. What do you mean about his 'globalism'? I think you are making strawman criticisms of him, can you elaborate or substantiate your claim regarding a George Soros-like position? I dont think you can. The spooky music and bizarre editing is a cheap trick. Misrepresenting his position is just plain lying.

—L4SERB0Y, *VOXIVERSITY: The Madness of Jordan Peterson*

This is a bit of a smear... for instance the clean your room spiel gives you control over a domain that is manageable. You discover you can operate in a manner to bring about control of a messy situation. You can then adopt this mentality to take on more complex issues with the use of structure & discipline in life. I found it quite profound. Then again maybe I just came up with that all on my own reading between the lines of his ramblings. Who knows?

—Donnie Grant, *VOXIVERSITY: The Madness of Jordan Peterson*

This video really exposes its author as a charlatan. If you are going to attempt to expose one of the worlds leading intellectuals, with thousands of hours of lectures online, 2 published, bestselling books and (if my memory serves me well) over 700 citations on published Psychology papers, in the top 0.1 percentile of clinical psychologists on the planet you're gonna need more than a 14 minute video :') You talk like he's just some dipshit with absolutely no idea what he's talking about. That requires a comical level of arrogance :')

—YT19890151, *VOXIVERSITY: The Madness of Jordan Peterson*

Hahaha! Cute video bro! JP would mop the floor with your face intellectually. Hell, his students would do it too! There's no argument here.

—Lucas Alvarez, *VOXIVERSITY: The Madness of Jordan Peterson*

While it's true that the rhetorical impact of the carefully selected quotes, the edits, the sound effects, and the music utilized in the video can hardly be described as fair, it is deeply ironic that the fans of a man who built his career on the intrinsically deceptive medium of video should complain about someone else using the same medium to effectively expose him.

After all, the most effective rhetoric points toward the truth, and all the producer's little tricks used to emphasize the message would not be anywhere nearly as effective if they were pushing falsehoods on the viewers. And I very much doubt that despite their complaints, Peterson's fans are going to be any happier when confronted by the detailed, reliably-sourced dialectic utilized in this book.

The truth is, despite its provocative title, the Voxiversity video barely began to even scratch the surface on the deeply troubling madness of Jordan Peterson.

Chapter 4

The Exodus

This whole Peterson thing has made me seriously evaluate how I was so easily tricked. I could have replaced his message that I held with such high regard with two sticky notes that say "clean your room" and "gulags are bad." Much respect for the early clarity on this one, Vox. I listen to people who are accurate and your batting average is revealing itself to be very high.

—Owen Benjamin

Despite the unhinged response of the true believers to the various videos, not all the comments were negative. In fact, it soon became clear that there was a real need for the videos, and that they were well worth doing, because they clearly managed to penetrate and dissipate the spell Jordan Peterson had cast on more than a few of his fans. With each and every video, more and more former fans and followers began to see through the charlatan and his spurious arguments, as the subsequent comments should suffice to demonstrate.

Excellent analysis. The clean room cult needs a collective slap in the face.

—Ut Naturalem, *DARKSTREAM: The Problem with Jordan Peterson*

*I was admittedly disappointed/confused when you first confronted
Peterson's jewish IQ claims. At this point, I need to thank you for
clarifying an impression that I've always had of him but never paid
any attention to due to his admirable sjw scalp count. This is turning
out to be very instructive.*

—Maxime Laneville, *DARKSTREAM: The Lunacy of
Jordan Peterson*

When I read in Dr. Peterson's, Maps of Meaning, *that he used to
bullshit all the time* when he was young, *I immediately became
suspicious of what I had laid my eyes on. I was an early supporter
of his, mostly because I've always found Carl Jung interesting. But
he's very hard to take seriously on anything else mostly because I don't
really know what he actually ever says. Nathan J. Robinson's article,
'The Intellectual We Deserve', was eye opening for me. He's definitely
figured Peterson out for me. Your little crusade is also entertaining and
consistent with what Nathan J. Robinson has said. This indicates to
me that people are finally onto something. Very interesting. I will
keep my eyes on this topic.*

—Luis F.R., *DARKSTREAM: Jordan Peterson is Bait
for the Broken*

*i like peterson, but in vox's defense, peterson often says that people will
actually tell you what's going on if you just listen to what they say—
which i'm assuming implies that people will unexpectedly convey the
truth if you take them literally. anyway, intuitively, i feel like vox is
actually on to something here, but i also think it's a bit harsh.*

—onseau, *DARKSTREAM: Why Jordan Peterson Doesn't
Take His Pills*

Initially, I respected the "idea of Jordan Peterson", but more and more, I realized that Peterson is rarely quotable... rarely clear. The "genius" can take something complicated and convey it in a simple manner. Though Peterson may package his ideas in florid semantics, most of his followers cannot even explain the man's ideas. Usually, they can only regurgitate buzz phrases like "Go clean your room", without fully understanding any direction beyond that initial step.

—Musical Cynic, *DARKSTREAM: Twelve Things I Learned From "12 Rules For Life"*

I was curious to see where your criticism of Jordan B. Peterson was going, now I get it, and you are, I think, correct. One has to listen and read his work in the light of what you explain here. Still interesting, but to be taken with a scoop of salt.

—piero san giorgio, *DARKSTREAM: The Core Purpose of Jordan Peterson*

i think im slowly understanding jordan petersons lies about truths. i didn't care about any of this crap till free speech became a question and obviously jordan peterson was in favor of it so maybe thats why he was so popular. im not as smart as you guys. his literary truths didn't make sense. it was confusing and since i thought he was smarter than me i trusted he was on to something. i guess it was bullshit. i think mid level intellects like me kind of put way to much trust in those we see to be smarter than us whether its fiction or truth.

—longcompton, *DARKSTREAM: Jordan Peterson is an "anti-Semitic dog-whistler" interesting - i had him pegged as a charlatan but it seems he may be substantially more sinister*

—salochin999, *DARKSTREAM: Jordan Peterson is a Globalist Shill*

Funny how the first video you did on Peterson, a big portion of your own audience were pissed off, but after the 3rd and 4th video, at that point you pretty much convinced us. At the time I still gave Peterson the benefit of the doubt but liked the points you were making. And then when you posted on your blog about Peterson's involvement in the UN, that entirely confirmed it for me.

—LRN_News, *DARKSTREAM: Seven Signs of an Intellectual Charlatan*

I can't believe I was a Peterson adherent. His followers are like SJW's. 'tsk tsk, communism hasn't been tried yet!' 'If I haven't read critiques of Peterson, they don't exist!'.

—The Don, *DARKSTREAM: An Apology to Jordan Peterson*

These Darkstreams have become my favourite videos on YouTube. Usually people with this level of competence dont have the time or interest to sit on front of the camera and upload stuff on the internet for free.

—Turkka Pahis, *DARKSTREAM: Jordan Peterson is a Free Speech Fake*

He taught me to stand up straight and clean my room. Now I have a clean room and great posture and a father figure my careerist mom never gave me. Now once that letter to Hogwarts arrives I'll be set...

—The View from Alfheim, *DARKSTREAM: 7 Answers to Jordan Peterson's Questions*

Wow. Case closed on the fraud Jordan Peterson.

—Dee Cue, *DARKSTREAM: An Alt-Right response to Jordan Peterson*

I used to be a Jordan Peterson fan and he definitely wasn't a gateway to the right for me. I've moved to the right not because of Peterson but because of Milo, Crowder, Trump and Vox.

—Commissar Carl, *DARKSTREAM: Gateways or Gatekeepers*

To be fair, you aren't just criticising him, you are pointing out the insanity of their hero. It's a tough pill to swallow when you make someone your hero and then you see what is going on. It's a lot less painful to call you jealous or an idiot or whatever than it is to admit you have been idolizing a crazy person.

—tarstarkusz, *DARKSTREAM: The Cultists Strike Back*

I was highly skeptical on your attacks against Peterson for a long while. It took me awhile to come around, but when you're right you're right, hat's off to you.

—Yordan Yordanov, *DARKSTREAM: The Miracles of St. Jordan Peterson*

I remember when I realized that Jordan Peterson is a charlatan. In the spring of 2017, Jordan Peterson made some videos talking about how impressed he was with Milo. How Milo is the "unstoppable court jester." How "bold" and "fast on his feet" and "fearless" Milo is. He said this with passion, and I thought it was actually pretty interesting. But then fast forward a year and Jordan Peterson is sitting in Aspen, Colorado with some phony journalist from the New York Times. She asserts out of the blue that Milo is a "racist." And what does Jordan Peterson do? He sits there and nods and acts like he agrees. Then he insists that he is not a "fan" of Milo's and tries to pretend like he doesn't even know who Milo is. The whole thing was a lie. Meanwhile, his whole talk involved the importance of not telling little lies. That is when I realized that Jordan Peterson is a charlatan.

—Tuduk Coba, *DARKSTREAM: Jordan Peterson stars as Wormtongue!*

The foam-flecked rantings of the Jordanetics cultists notwithstanding, even the much-criticized Voxiversity video, with its hundreds of dislikes, also received hundreds of likes and positive comments from viewers who found the case that it presented to not only be convincing, but conclusive. Here are five examples of viewers whose reaction to the video was a positive one.

Great use of rhetoric in this video by Vox and his producer. No wonder most Peterson fanboys are so triggered by it. And still, were they to actually think about what is being said and verify they would have no choice than to acknowledge that Vox is not lying. Deep down they know this. So they try to discredit as hit piece, smear etc. so they don't have to face the painful truth: Irregardless of how useful or enjoyable they have found Peterson's content to be, the man is still a disingenuous fraud and fake intellectual.

—Wenzel, *VOXIVERSITY: The Madness of Jordan Peterson*

I have watched Dr. Peterson rise to 'fame' over the last two years and found his work thought-provoking with no negative word against him. However, listening to this I must admit that his speedy rise to fame and connection with agents from Hollywood cause me to pause. Through book sales reaching great heights, world tours and growing notoriety, I've wondered about the bigger message and just where it fits with the global plan that too many are oblivious to. Thank you for giving me more food for thought.

—Charlotte Nilpart, *VOXIVERSITY: The Madness of Jordan Peterson*

Thanks for discrediting this guy. I almost got sucked into the hype but something in my spirit said steer clear. You are giving concrete reasons of why he is bad news.

—Big Black Bear, *VOXIVERSITY: The Madness of Jordan Peterson*

How on Earth can an alleged genius devote so much time speaking about the Bible, whether he's read it or not, without ever pondering his own belief about whether or not Christ was resurrected? That's a key component to Christian faith. I could have even accepted an "I'm still not sure" as an answer. But playing coy about "How you define Jesus"?

—vtmegrad98, *VOXIVERSITY: The Madness of Jordan Peterson*

Well formed and coherent. Looking at Peterson through a more coherent and congruent lens exposes him for us to see who he is.

—Steve K, *VOXIVERSITY: The Madness of Jordan Peterson*

A common theme among ex-Peterson fans is a sense of bewilderment over how they could have been taken in so easily, and so completely, by such an obvious charlatan. The reason, I think, is a combination of the considerable effort that Jordan Peterson puts into selling his false image with his almost sociopathic lack of shame.

Think about how ridiculous you would feel if you were to publicly claim that you had not slept at all for 25 days after drinking a single glass of apple cider. What would have to go through your head in order for such a claim to strike you as credible, let alone something that would you make you look good?

The world record for a confirmed lack of sleep is 264.4 hours, or 11 days and 25 minutes, set by Randy Gardner in 1964, so it's entirely obvious that Jordan Peterson could not possibly have gone 600 hours without sleep, whether he was drinking apple cider or smoking methamphetamine. And yet, he still has not retracted the claim he made to that effect in July 2018 on the Joe Rogan show.

"I didn't sleep that month for 25 days. I didn't sleep at all for 25 days."

"What? How is that possible?"

"I'll tell you how it's possible: You lay in bed frozen in something approximating terror for eight hours. And then you get up."

This is straightforward nonsense. And yet, Peterson does not even hesitate to produce this story as evidence in support of his new all-meat diet.

Chapter 5

Who Is the Real Jordan Peterson?

*I think I have discovered something that no one else has any idea about,
and I'm not sure I can do it justice. Its scope is so broad that I can see
only parts of it clearly at one time, and it is exceedingly difficult to set
down comprehensibly in writing.*

—Dr. Jordan Peterson

Pathological liar or prophet-philosopher? Shaman or charlatan? Hoax
or healer? Great intellect or grandiose pretender? These are the questions this book is intended to conclusively answer for even the most
skeptical reader.

If you are a fan of Peterson's and you are still standing by your man, I
expect that more than a few objections to my assertions about him are
likely to have occurred to you. In anticipation of these objections, I have
summarized those that are most often made in thousands of critical,
often angry, comments and emails that I have been sent by Peterson
enthusiasts responding to my various videos and blog posts. Some of
them are specious, others are sincere, but regardless, I have responded
to them.

**Objection 1: Jordan Peterson is a complex thinker with a Platonic
approach that is easily misunderstood by those who don't carefully
follow him. You just don't understand him.**

I answer that, It is true that Peterson is inclined to excessive wordiness
and run-on sentences, his references are often obscure, and the examples

he provides are frequently too loosely connected and meandering for the average person to easily follow. But the nebulous word salad Peterson customarily presents in lieu of logical arguments is not at all typical of a genius-level intellect, to the contrary, it is much more commonly observed among academic poseurs who wish to be mistaken for one.

If you have actually read the great thinkers of whom Peterson is almost entirely ignorant, one thing that will often strike you is the intense clarity of their thought processes. Their genius stems from the way in which they enlighten the reader, from the way they turn dark chaos into orderly light. They do not confuse, to the contrary, they clarify.

As an exercise, compare the following four sentences, all of which are more complex than the norm these days. I ran each of them through the Gunning-Fog Index, a weighted average of the number of words per sentence, and the number of long words per word. The index provides a number that is supposed to indicate that the text can be understood by someone who left full-time education at a later age than the number; the higher the number, the more complicated the text. But it's really just an objective measure of textual complexity.

1. We must be able to employ persuasion, just as strict reasoning can be employed, on opposite sides of a question, not in order that we may in practice employ it in both ways (for we must not make people believe what is wrong), but in order that we may see clearly what the facts are, and that, if another man argues unfairly, we on our part may be able to confute him. (GFI 31.6)

2. In like manner the poet with his words and phrases may be said to lay on the colours of the several arts, himself understanding their nature only enough to imitate them; and other people, who are as ignorant as he is, and judge only from his words, imagine that if he speaks of cobbling, or of military tactics, or of anything else, in metre and harmony and rhythm, he speaks very well—

such is the sweet influence which melody and rhythm by nature have. (GFI 21.9)

3. The great dramatists and religious thinkers of the world have been able to grasp this fact, at least implicitly, and to transmit it in story and image; modern analytic thinkers and existential theorists have attempted to abstract these ideas upward into "higher consciousness," and to present them in logical and purely semantic form. (GFI 18.2)

4. We have considered that students in this doctrine have not seldom been hampered by what they have found written by other authors, partly on account of the multiplication of useless questions, articles, and arguments, partly also because those things that are needful for them to know are not taught according to the order of the subject matter, but according as the plan of the book might require, or the occasion of the argument offer, partly, too, because frequent repetition brought weariness and confusion to the minds of readers. (40.2)

Were you able to distinguish the Peterson quote from the Aquinas, the Aristotle, and the Plato quotes? If you noticed, the Peterson sentence, which is the third sentence, is considerably shorter and less structurally complex than the other three examples, but it is also observably less clear than them. Whereas the Aristotle sentence in particular is rich with meaning, as it implies a vital distinction between rhetoric and dialectic that many today have trouble grasping even when it is explained to them in no little detail, but nevertheless clarifies the relevant point for the reader, the Peterson sentence unnecessarily complicates what is a fairly simple and straightforward observation about the mythopoetic human response to the concepts of good and evil.

And yes, the GFI on that last sentence was a respectable 36.3. But it wasn't actually that hard to follow or understand, was it? Complexity is neither ambiguity nor nebulosity, and insight does not require complexity. Also, in case you're interested, the authors of the four sentences, in order, were: Aristotle, Plato/Socrates, Peterson, Aquinas.

Now, I am no Aristotle or Aquinas, but I do happen to be one of the bestselling political philosophers alive, I was a National Merit Finalist, I was a member of Mensa, and I possess an IQ that falls between the third and fourth standard deviations. So, if I can't muddle my way through the intricate complexities of Jordan Peterson's philosophy and comprehend its true meaning, how likely is it that you have done so? Are you really certain that you have done so correctly? Please note that I'm not offering myself as an authority in a logically fallacious *argumentum ab auctoritate* here, I'm merely pointing to the obvious probabilities involved.

Furthermore, I have noticed that if you ask four different Peterson fans about what he means about any given subject, you usually get four different answers, at least two of which are intrinsically contradictory, and none of which actually correspond to what Peterson himself says. Here are four different takes on Peterson's definition of truth, each of which has been helpfully explained in some detail by a fan.

1. If you are going to go for a definition of truth that JBP subscribes to, one should probably go with the one that JBP mentions: pragmatism and the book that he recommends: *The Metaphysical Club* by Louis Menand.

2. Peterson subscribes to a pragmatist version of the Coherence theory of truth…. On Peterson's stated theory of truth, an idea can be thought to be true (or false) at a "micro" or "proximal" level—e.g., at the level of a scientific experiment, or at some other level that does not take the morality of the idea into account—yet actually be false (or true) at a "macro" or "distal" level that includes a consideration of whether the idea is pro-survival or anti-survival (i.e., good or evil). For Peterson, it is the macro/distal level—the level that includes a consideration of the morality of the effects of an idea—that determines the

idea's truth or falsity. For Peterson, the standard of the moral truth—i.e., of the goodness—of an idea is that the effect of the using or acting upon an idea is ultimately pro-survival (of the individual, or a number of individuals, or all of humanity).

3. Peterson isn't so much ascribing to a coherence theory of truth, its more a pragmatic form of Nietzsche's Perspectivism. Perspectivism would hold that there are no objective metaphysical truths, or if there are they are completely unknowable so it doesn't matter anyways. This is a bit rooted in subjective idealism and phenomenology and existentialism, the idea that reality is only the perceptions of human consciousness and does not in any way independently exist. And then you add on the Will to Power and the human Will being the central force in the universe, and it all spirals downhill from there. We are talking about a literal madman here, after all. So, on that basis, every Will is subject to its own perspectives, its own way of interpreting its perceptions. Therefore, we have no choice but to conclude that no truth is absolute and objective, for any such truth would need to be capable of transcending all limits on perception.

4. My understanding is that Peterson argues that human interaction and agency works through logos and narrative, and so can be considered a separate system from objective, scientific reality. Following from that, he says that the narrative structure is embedded in the psyche, and its archetypes can embody psychological truths that he considers more meaningful than scientific truths.

All of them cannot be right. It's literally impossible. So what does Peterson himself say about the definition of truth, in those words that he has very, very carefully selected?

I don't think facts are necessarily true. So I don't think these scientific facts, even if they're correct from within the domain that they were generated, I don't think that that necessarily makes them true. And I know that I am gerrymandering the definition of truth, but I'm doing that on purpose. Your truth is something only you can tell, based as it is on the unique circumstances of your life.

—Dr. Jordan Peterson

In summary, I would suggest that I understand Jordan Peterson very well indeed, especially in light of the direction provided by three great thinkers who are considerably more clear on the subject of truth.

To say that that which is, is not or that which is not is, is a falsehood; and to say that that which is, is and that which is not is not, is true.

—Aristotle

If it be not fitting, do it not. If it be not true, speak it not.

—Marcus Aurelius

Let your Yes be Yes, and your No, No. For whatever is more than these is from the evil one.

—Jesus Christ of Nazareth

Objection 2: The 12 Rules are designed to be a la carte. Just keep what you find useful and discard the rest.

I answer that, There is a considerable amount of valuable knowledge that originates from a wide variety of people of the most dubious morals. To reject information out of hand on the sole basis of its source is to commit the Genetic Fallacy, after all, you can almost certainly learn something useful about both architecture and security systems from a burglar.

You can certainly discover something useful about propaganda by reading *The Dictatorship of the Proletariat and the Renegade Kautsky*. Saul Alinsky's *Rules for Radicals* are invaluable to those who would understand and resist the tactics of the radical Left. Many ex-Scientologists explain that it was the bits of useful advice in L. Ron Hubbard's *Dianetics* that made it so difficult for them to quit, even long after the religion that is built upon those foundations had stopped making sense to them. You can pick out any number of points from *12 Rules* that seem okay. But the problem with this defense is that the book itself promotes something much bigger, and something far more evil, than any superficial observation about posture can possibly absolve.

Of course, this is clouded by the madness, ignorance and solipsism evident throughout the book, but underneath it all is a very specific message, a message that would not sell nearly as well if it were expressed clearly from the outset. By the end of this book, the antidote it provides to chaos of Jordanetics should make that hidden message obvious.

Objection 3: You are just jealous of Jordan Peterson's success!

I answer that, If you look at Jordan Peterson's life, even by his own account there is virtually nothing to envy except perhaps his bank account. The man is a clinically depressed pathological liar who has written all of two books, both of which are meandering, incoherent tosses of word salad. I don't even know how many books I've published, something like 15 not including the various comics books, and reviewers of my epic fantasy series *Arts of Dark and Light* usually put it somewhere in between George Martin's *A Song of Ice and Fire* and J.R.R. Tolkien's *The Lord of the Rings*.

As a writer, yeah, I'll take that.

And no father would ever envy what Jordan Peterson has been through with his daughter's various ailments, which have been legitimately horrific since childhood. Envy the man? To the contrary, I pity him tremendously. There is a very good reason why he subscribes to the idea that life is suffering; suffering and frustrated ambition is virtually all he has ever known.

My childhood friend didn't kill himself. I distrust the media and regularly decline interview requests. I have refused every single speaking engagement that has been offered to me for the last 17 years despite having had no shortage of them as a nationally syndicated columnist. My band Psykosonik didn't even go on tour back in the day; the idea of traveling around the world to perform in public for complete strangers is about as close to my idea of Hell on Earth as it gets. The only venues we played were the Minneapolis clubs we already frequented: First Avenue, 7th Street Entry, the Perimeter, the Living Room, and Glam Slam.

If I was jealous of anyone's intellectual success, it would be Nicolas Nassim Taleb, who has far more money than Jordan Peterson, has written more bestsellers, and whose work will last far longer than Jordan Peterson's. Taleb, or Sean McVay, who at 31 is already the head coach of the Los Angeles Rams. I think I would have been a good NFL coach, if I'd gone that route.

Also, my bestselling computer game sold six million units and Psykosonik recorded four *Billboard* Top 40 Club Chart hits. I genuinely don't give a quantum of a damn about Jordan Peterson's success, such as it is, and neither jealousy nor envy are the reason I have turned my baleful eye upon the man and his teachings.

And finally, for the sake of all the involuntary celibates in the Jordan Peterson fan club, I'll spell out the conclusive evidence as mercifully as possible: men with pretty wives do not envy men with not-pretty wives. Let's just leave it at that.

My motivation is perfectly straightforward. The man is a charlatan and his fans insisted on repeatedly telling me not to believe my lying eyes. Hence this book.

Objection 4: I am an intelligent person. How could a smart person like me possibly be fooled by the esoteric incoherence of a lunatic?

I answer that, Jordan Peterson's intellectual con game is less about fooling the casual observer, and more about disarming and subtly misleading the intelligent one. It is actually quite easy for people of above average intelligence to be convinced to place their confidence in those who successfully demonstrate that they are even more intelligent. Peterson presents himself as a thoughtful man of gentle, honest, careful speech. He has a very high level of verbal intelligence, which he utilizes to assemble his carefully constructed matrix of lies and rationalize the bizarre behavioral mechanisms he requires in order to function on a daily basis. He has written his bestselling book for a reader of above-average intelligence, and in doing so, has gone to considerable effort in order to conceal his incoherence and his intellectual crimes.

The *12 Rules for Life* is a murder mystery disguised as a self-help book and the intended victim is you.

In short, an outright fool is far less likely to be taken in by Peterson's *12 Rules* than the intelligent truth-seeker who is smart enough to assume that a book marketed as self-help actually focuses on providing self-help advice and techniques, rather than a dangerous reliance upon occult mind control practices. One of the weaknesses of intelligent people is they have a greater ability to rationalize away their instinctive responses to things that don't make sense.

But the genuine truth-seeker will eventually discover Peterson's habitual deceit, because it is woven throughout his philosophy. Although the honest reader may not come to a full understanding of the evil nature of the esotericism that underlies that philosophy, he will inevitably conclude that he has no choice but to turn away from both the man and his works.

Objection 5: He has helped so many people and he does so much good for the broken, confused young men of today. He even cries for them!

I answer that, There is no credible metric by which Jordan Peterson can be said to have helped anyone, except perhaps to lighten their wallets. The fact that he sheds crocodile tears while charging unemployed young men $300 to shake his hand is justification for condemning him as a con man, not beatifying him as some sort of living secular saint.

In his bio, Peterson claims to have helped over 100,000 people by means of his "self-authoring suite", the name of which alone should be sufficient to get your skeptical antennae twitching.

Objection 6: Assuming for the moment that Peterson's Rules are deceptive. How does he pull off the alleged scam?

I answer that, There are a couple of things to consider. First, understand that Peterson divulges, in bits and pieces, some unvarnished truths about himself, but he does not do it in an honest and straightforward manner. By compartmentalizing some of the more untrustworthy aspects of his own nature and by presenting them as examples of normal human failure, he attempts to minimize them. In fact, he's more than a little successful in doing so, as very few of his readers tend to pick up on his self-admitted ugly qualities on their first reading of *12 Rules for Life*.

Peterson is, by his own admission, a non-confrontational coward by nature. As a child, he felt free to snipe at a friend of his while under the shield of his own father's classroom, but begged, pleaded, and successfully fled the same friend when the friend tried to confront him about it, even though it resulted in the death of the friendship.

I had skipped a grade in school, and was, in addition, small for my age. Rene was a big, smart, good-looking kid, and he was tough. We were in grade six together, in a class taught by my father. Rene was caught chewing gum. 'Rene,' said my father, 'spit that gum out. You

look like a cow.' 'Ha, ha,' I laughed, under my breath. 'Rene the cow.'
Rene might have been a cow, but there was nothing wrong with his
hearing. 'Peterson,' he said, 'after school—you're dead.'

...After school...[w]e circled around the bikes, him on one side, me
on the other. We were characters in a 'Keystone Cops' short. As long
as I kept circling, he couldn't catch me, but my strategy couldn't work
forever. I yelled out that I was sorry, but he wasn't mollified. His pride
was hurt, and he wanted me to pay.

I crouched down and hid behind some bikes, keeping an eye on Rene.
'Rene,' I yelled. 'I'm sorry I called you a cow. Let's quit fighting.' He
started to approach me again. I said, 'Rene, I am sorry I said that.
Really. And I still want to go to the movie with you.' This wasn't just
a tactic. I meant it.

—12 Rules for Life

This was not a singular event. When Peterson was a young father,
another child abused his own daughter, whose symptoms from a de-
generative arthritic condition had already begun to appear. The boy
repeatedly stepped, deliberately, on her hands on the monkey bars,
yet Peterson could not bring himself to confront the child, and even
decades later, resorts to petty fantasy in lieu of action.

She was playing on the monkey bars, hanging in mid-air. A partic-
ularly provocative little monster of about the same age was standing
above her on the same bar she was gripping. I watched him move
towards her. Our eyes locked. He slowly and deliberately stepped
on her hands, with increasing force, over and over, as he stared me
down. He knew exactly what he was doing. Up yours, Daddy-O—
that was his philosophy. He had already concluded that adults were
contemptible, and that he could safely defy them. (Too bad, then,
that he was destined to become one.) That was the hopeless future

his parents had saddled him with. To his great and salutary shock, I
picked him bodily off the playground structure, and threw him thirty
feet down the field. No I didn't. I just took my daughter somewhere
else. But it would have been better for him if I had.

—12 Rules for Life

There are a number of similar incidents of Peterson's conflict-
avoidance, including refraining from correcting a toddler after he struck
Peterson's child with a heavy toy truck, and failing to address a colleague's psychological and physical negligence of her child who was left
in his care. He violates about half his own rules in order to distract a
drunken neighbor from shaking him down for money. In pieces, these
little stories are designed to illustrate something about the individual
rules, but gathered in one place, it becomes far more clear: Peterson is
unable to confront people, even when circumstances clearly deem such
confrontation appropriate.

He condemns this sort of behavior in a powerful way:

If you flick your two-year-old with your finger just after he smacks the
baby on the head with a wooden block, he will get the connection,
and be at least somewhat less willing to smack her again in the future.
That seems like a good outcome. He certainly won't conclude that he
should hit her more, using the flick of his mother's finger as an example.
He's not stupid. He's just jealous, impulsive and not very sophisticated.
And how else are you going to protect this younger sibling? If you
discipline ineffectively, then the baby will suffer. Maybe for years. The
bullying will continue, because you won't do a damn thing to stop
it. You'll avoid the conflict that's necessary to establish peace. You'll
turn a blind eye. And then later, when the younger child confronts
you (maybe even in adulthood), you'll say, "I never knew it was like
that." You just didn't want to know. So, you didn't. You just rejected
the responsibility of discipline and justified it with a continual show

of your niceness. Every gingerbread house has a witch inside it that
devours children.

—12 Rules for Life

When you put the multiple instances of Peterson's own struggle
with lifelong passivity together with his condemnation of passivity it
becomes clear: most of the 12 Rules that he recommends to the reader
are actually rules conceived to correct his own personal persistent weaknesses. His strongest arguments tend to be autobiographical attacks on
his own failings.

Secondly, Peterson is sloppy with his scholarship and citations. He
makes broad, sweeping generalizations based off a single citation that
actually indicates a more specific purpose. It is easy to gloss over one or
two of these citational crimes as mere error, but as they stack up over
the course of both *12 Rules for Life* and *Maps of Meaning* it gradually
becomes clear that there is a purposeful pattern behind these errors.

**Objection 7: Jordan Peterson is a well-respected academic and an
internationally bestselling author who is noted for his brilliant
intellect and his common sense wisdom. How can you possibly
suggest that he is some sort of con man or something even worse?**

I answer that, Jordan Peterson is also complete whack job. He is
mentally ill. But he is also intelligent, and his 12-Rule Path is a method
he has developed to help him navigate the complexities of the sane
world without abandoning his delusions. He is a high-functioning
madman, but he is a madman all the same.

A high IQ and the ability to function well in human society, even to
succeed in it, is no indicator of sanity. There are convicted serial killers
with IQs that made them eligible for membership in Mensa; Ted Bundy
even had a degree in psychology from the University of Washington.

The troubling relationship of the 12 Rules to dark esoteric literature
is impossible for those who are sufficiently familiar with the material to

ignore. But even the most casual Peterson acquaintance, whether he has read Peterson's books or not, has been provided with an abundance of clues indicating that something is fundamentally wrong with the man:

> *The house had been gutted by Tammy, his wife, and himself, and turned into perhaps the most fascinating and shocking middle-class home I had seen. They had art, some carved masks, and abstract portraits, but they were overwhelmed by a huge collection of Socialist Realist paintings of Lenin and the early Communists commissioned by the USSR.... Paintings lionizing the Soviet revolutionary spirit completely filled every single wall, the ceilings, even the bathrooms. The paintings were not there because Jordan had any totalitarian sympathies, but because he wanted to remind himself of something he knew he and everyone would rather forget: that over a hundred milllion people were murdered in the name of utopia. It took getting used to, this semi-haunted house "decorated" by a delusion that had practically destroyed mankind.*

> —*12 Rules for Life,* Dr. Norman Doidge, page xii

It may be understandable for a man obsessed with preventing the next Holocaust, whose life is dedicated to fighting the historical tyranny represented by Communism, to keep some tokens around to remind himself to "never forget." But we are told that Peterson's *own family home* has been transformed into a grotesque fetish-altar to Communism! The ceilings? Every single wall? Should someone so concerned about oppression really require this level of wallowing in historical propaganda to remind him that it is bad? Of course not! Would a dedicated hunter of serial killers ever decorate his house with the clown portraits of John Wayne Gacy, just to remind himself that serial killing is a bad thing?

Peterson shares a number of his dreams and visions throughout both *12 Rules for Life* and *Maps of Meaning.* The mere fact of their inclusion should give any Christian reader pause, while the significance that Peterson ascribes to them should trouble every sane reader regardless of his religious beliefs. Although it is no surprise that a Jungian psychologist would pay attention to his own dreams, the esoteric elements described in these visions can hardly be missed by anyone.

> *I dreamt one night during this period that I was suspended in midair, clinging to a chandelier, many stories above the ground, directly under the dome of a massive cathedral. The people on the floor below were distant and tiny. There was a great expanse between me and any wall—and even the peak of the dome itself.... My dream placed me at the center of Being itself, and there was no escape.*

—*12 Rules for Life*

Contrary to his usual practice, Peterson helpfully interprets his own dream here, explaining:

> *The centre is occupied by the individual. The centre is marked by the cross, as X marks the spot. Existence at that cross is suffering and transformation—and that fact, above all, needs to be voluntarily accepted. It is possible to transcend slavish adherence to the group and its doctrines and, simultaneously, to avoid the pitfalls of its opposite extreme, nihilism. It is possible, instead, to find sufficient meaning in individual consciousness and experience."*

—*12 Rules for Life*

Peterson's philosophy shares a number of elements with some of history's more notorious spiritualists, including L. Ron Hubbard, Aleister Crowley and Helena Blavatsky. His *12 Rules for Life* rely upon some of their fundamental tenets, although, again, he hides those tenets beneath commonplace metaphors and large quantities of word-salad. Over the course of the book, however, you will gradually begin to recognize when he is attempting to sneak one of them past you.

But again, you need not be familiar with the terminology of the occult to recognize when you are dealing with a madman. It's hard to decide which is crazier, the following dream that Peterson relates, or the fact that he actually decided to put it down in writing and share it with the world.

> *I dreamed I saw my maternal grandmother sitting by the bank of a swimming pool, which was also a river. In real life, she had been a victim of Alzheimer's disease and had regressed to a semi-conscious state. In the dream, as well, she had lost her capacity for self-control. Her genital region was exposed, dimly; it had the appearance of a thick mat of hair. She was stroking herself, absentmindedly. She walked over to me, with a handful of pubic hair compacted into something resembling a large artist's paintbrush. She pushed this at my face. I raised my arm, several times, to deflect her hand; finally, unwilling to hurt her, or interfere with her any further, I let her have her way. She stroked my face with the brush, gently, and said, like a child, "Isn't it soft?" I looked at her ruined face and said, "Yes, Grandma, it's soft."*

> *—Maps of Meaning: The Architecture of Belief*

Grandma is not the only family member about whom Peterson dreams in a distinctly sexual manner. He also dreams about his cousin Diane, who he describes as being the most beautiful woman he had ever seen in waking life.

> *Some dogs emerged, out from under the basement stairs, where they had inexplicably taken residence. They were standing upright, on their hind legs. They were thin, like greyhounds, and had pointed noses. They looked like creatures of ritual—like Anubis, from the Egyptian tombs. They were carrying plates in front of them, which contained*

pieces of seared meat. They wanted to trade the meat for the cans. I took a plate. In the center of it was a circular slab of flesh four inches in diameter and one inch thick, foully cooked, oily, with a marrow bone in the center of it. Where did it come from?

I had a terrible thought. I rushed downstairs to my cousin. The dogs had butchered her, and were offering the meat to the survivors of the disaster.

—Maps of Meaning: The Architecture of Belief

Forget accepting advice on how to live your life from this lunatic. Jordan Peterson is the creepy relative that all the teenage girls in the family do their best to avoid during the holidays because he stares at them too long.

Objection 8: You claim that Jordan Peterson has been misleading me. How do I know that you aren't the one who is lying about him?

I answer that, If there is one thing for which I am known, it is that I do not lie in public or on the Internet. I am sometimes misinformed. I sometimes get things wrong. I am certainly aware of Sun Tzu's directive to mislead one's enemies. But I do not deceive my readers and I do not lie to them.

Possibly the greatest compliment I have ever been paid was by a critic who does not like me and does not agree with my politics. However, after pointing that out, he went on to say, "Vox doesn't lie. If he said the sky was green, I wouldn't even bother to look out the window to check."

It's not because I am some paragon of Christian virtue. It's not because I am any more morally upstanding than you are. I'm just as prone to self-serving spin and narrative as the average man, although not to the extent of a pathological liar like Jordan Peterson. It's merely that, as a nationally syndicated columnist, I learned early on that my every word would be carefully scrutinized by my worst enemies, hundreds of them, each looking for some sort of error or inconsistency that could be used against me.

I have written 535 columns and over 20,000 blog posts. Prior to my decision to stop granting requests for interviews, I had spent dozens of hours of being asked questions by friendly and hostile interviewers. And one of the more common lamentations of the journalists who tried to write hit pieces about me is that I never gave them anything they could use to disqualify or discredit me.

The only way to do that is to tell the truth. The only way you can reliably keep your story straight over an extended period of time is to tell the truth each and every time. The only way to avoid spending your days and nights in an agony of anxiety over being found out and exposed is to always tell the truth.

Now, imagine that you are trying to escape a labyrinth in which you are trapped. You finally arrive at two doors. One door is a trap and it leads to certain death. The other is the exit and it leads to freedom. In front of each door is a living gargoyle, one which will only tell the truth, and the other will only tell lies.

If you ask them which door leads to freedom, then both will reply in the same way: "The door behind me."

If you ask them which door leads to death, then both will reply: "The door behind the other gargoyle."

However, there is a question that will reveal the truth to you: "If I were to ask *the other gargoyle* which door leads to freedom, what would *he* say?"

If nothing else, this book should provide you with the information required to allow you to determine for yourself whether Jordan Peterson is lying, or if I am lying about him.

Chapter 6

The Lobster of Mediocrity

He has built a case on false facts and distortions of general observations from the scientific literature. He has not demonstrated anything about socio-cultural constructions. Not only does he get the evidence wrong, he can't construct any kind of logical argument.... It's appalling the degree to which this man is asserting nonsense with such smug confidence. This man is lying to you and if you fall for any of it you should be embarrassed.

—Dr. P.Z. Myers

Rule 1: Stand up straight with your shoulders back.

Good posture is certainly a good thing. Slouching and other forms of bad posture are not only interpreted to one's detriment by other human beings, they are physically detrimental. At first glance, there appears to be nothing but a reminder of basic parental wisdom in Peterson's first rule. But in the lengthy chapter that purports to further illuminate this rule, he hardly mentions human posture at all. That is because the directive to stand up straight with your shoulders back is nothing more than the truth bait set at the back of an elaborate metaphorical cage for the reader.

The metaphor for the chapter begins with lobsters. Peterson illustrates the primal nature of the creatures as they jockey for social position within their dominance hierarchy. The winning lobster, who attracts the best and most females, gains material advantage and social position, quite literally stands tall in comparison with his fellow lobsters.

Then, arguing that human social order predates humanity because we are direct inheritors of the social hierarchy of crustaceans and share common ancestry with them, Peterson asserts that the Dominance Hierarchy is the primary architecture of society. Peterson's reliance upon evolutionary theory here reveals his ignorance of it, for as biologist P.Z. Myers points out, his idea is not consistent with current evolutionary history.

We diverged from lobsters in evolutionary history about 350 million years ago. Common ancestor? No, that is ridiculous! 350 million years ago puts us in the early Carboniferous. Does he think lobsters evolved from sharks?

—Dr. P.Z. Myers, *Jordan Peterson & the Lobster*

As I learned in the course of writing this book, no one thinks less of Jordan Peterson than the subject-matter expert into whose wheelhouse Humanity's Greatest Thinker has deigned to briefly enter. Peterson speaks, and writes, with smug assurance and pseudo-erudition about everything from evolutionary biology and Christian theology to the works of Friedrich Nietzsche and Carl Jung, but the biologists recognize that he knows nothing about evolution, theologians can hardly miss his ignorance of Christian theology, the Nietzsche experts recognize that he doesn't understand Nietzsche's philosophy, and the Jung experts are well aware that he doesn't get Jung right either.

Also, as it happens, Dr. Myers actually minimized Peterson's evolutionary error. As one of his colleagues helpfully pointed out, arthropod and chordate lineages existed as distinct phyla during the Cambrian era and the current estimate for divergence between the two is around 800 million years ago, assuming that you subscribe to the Theorum of

Evolution by (probably) Natural Selection, Biased Mutation, Genetic Drift, and Gene Flow, anyhow.

But to return to the first rule, we are informed that everyone has a place in the Dominance Hierarchy, and Peterson describes a general scale from one at the top to ten at the bottom. And it is here that he identifies the primary audience for his twelve rules: the bottom feeders.

If you are a low-status ten, by contrast, male or female, you have nowhere to live (or nowhere good.) Your food is terrible, when you're not going hungry. You're in poor physical and mental condition. You're of minimal romantic interest to anyone, unless they are as desperate as you. You are more likely to fall ill, age rapidly, and die young, with few, if any, to mourn you.

—12 Rules for Life

Life is bad at the bottom. The bottom of the dominance hierarchy is a dangerous and terrible place. Peterson's description of the life at the bottom is the first picture of the dread chaos to which his rules are promised to be the antidote.

Peterson observes that the lowly ten in the hierarchy is likely to be bullied and that bullying can have long-term effects after the bullying has stopped, which is certainly true. Peterson argues that although there are those who can't stop the bullying against them due to relative personal weakness, there are also many instances when a bullied person could stop it by simply standing up to the bully, yet fail to do so.

If you say no, early in the cycle of oppression, and you mean what you say ... then the scope for oppression on the part of the oppressor will remain properly bounded and limited. The forces of tyranny expand inexorably to fill the space made available for their existence.

—12 Rules for Life

In other words, stand up for yourself and you can stop the bully. And to a degree, some victims of oppression can limit their suffering by resisting their oppressors. By taking up one's cross of Being and casting dead, rigid and too tyrannical Order back into the Chaos in which it was generated, the man who stands up for himself can be his own hero, find his adventure, accept the terrible burden of the World, embark upon his spiritual destiny, and thereby reach the Enlightenment of Balance.

Peterson suggests something very interesting here, namely, that chaos is both where the bottom folk are bullied without mercy and the source of tyranny. However, with his customary inconsistency, he has also made it very clear that tyrants dwell at the top of the Dominance Hierarchy. He describes two realms in detail, and he only alludes to a third realm that sits between them.

- **ORDER:** *Domain of Tyrants. The top of the Dominance Hierarchy.*
- **MIDDLE WAY:** *Domain of Balance. The more perfect Order.*
- **CHAOS:** *Domain of the Oppressed. The bottom of the Dominance Hierarchy.*

Although Peterson does not give a name to the social area to which one should aspire when standing up and assuming the burden of the world within the Dominance Hierarchy, he makes it clear that the two regions at the bottom and at the top are the areas to avoid. As he does not name it, for now we shall call it the Middle Way.

Like Dante's Inferno, Peterson's Dominance Hierarchy appears to have a number of circles or levels through which some special people are capable of transmigrating, while others are condemned permanently to their assigned realm.

As Above, So Below

But this is where the advice to stand up straight begins to go sideways. If the Dominance Hierarchy is a primordial order and too much order is tyranny, is it not wrong to advance up the hierarchy all the way to the top? Is that not the route to the temptations of tyranny? If the victim of oppression has power over his oppressor merely by resisting oppression, at what point does the lowly ten's survival and advancement transform into the bullying and oppression that is inevitable in the Domain of Tyrants?

Peterson is evidently aware of this problem. Although he encourages his readers to climb out of the bottom, Peterson also warns directly against rising too high.

It means casting dead, rigid and too tyrannical order back into the chaos in which it was generated; it means withstanding the ensuing uncertainty, and establishing, in consequence, a better, more meaningful and more productive order.

To the casual reader, it may appear as if Peterson is saying that the tyranny of Order is the promised antidote to Chaos, but that isn't true. What he is actually doing is referring to a third realm. He's finally identifying the Middle Way, but he's giving it what is the confusingly misleading name of a better and more productive Order.

So, he's established the Chaos of the Bottom, and we know the "dead, rigid and too tyrannical order" comes from that, and that it is located at the top of the Dominance Hierarchy. So this new better order that he believes can be brought about by "standing up with your shoulders back" has to exist between those two extreme and inhospitable poles. Later in the book, he finally acknowledges that this area is, indeed, more appropriately called The Middle Way.

But Peterson, a man who claims to choose his words very, very precisely, is egregiously imprecise here in the first chapter. Why does he call what is quite obviously the middle by a misleading term that is bound to confuse the average reader, especially when he has already defined Order as something else and identified it as the negative, tyrannical pinnacle of the dominance hierarchy?

This is one of the earliest cases of Jordan's Clintonian tendency to swap definitions as it suits him at the moment. He defined a term, Order, as being at the top of the Dominance Hierarchy, but has now introduced a new definition for an even better Order that is the area between Bottom and Top, between Hell and Heaven, between the Underworld and the Elite, an area between that is decidedly not at the top where the other Order is. It may help to think of Order as sort of evil twin of the middle, more productive Order, because Peterson apparently intends for you to confuse the two in this rule.

He is a Jungian clinical psychologist, and playing fast-and-loose in this way with the definitions of terms is a technique that he employs with some frequency, so it is always informative to keep a very careful watch on his terms and definitions.

It is important to note that Jordan Peterson tends to lean heavily on evolutionary psychology when drawing out his extended illustrations. This tendency to Darwinize man's impressions of nature for insights into how a modern man should conduct himself in the 21st century has serious problems, which the anthropologist Christopher Hallpike has demonstrated in considerable detail. It is possible that this heavy reliance upon evolutionary pseudo-science stems from Peterson's inability to reliably utilize the plain meaning of normal words, but I think it is more likely that Peterson simply believes that putting a scientific veneer on his flights of historical fancy gives them more credibility.

"Evolutionary psychologists", who claim that our human abilities and traits are very specific adaptations to the problems of pre-historic life on the savannah in East Africa, have not faced up to the fact that we know virtually nothing about what this life involved, about the social relations and organisation of our ancestors in those remote epochs, and still less about their mental capacities.... Normal science proceeds from the known to the unknown, but evolutionary psychology tries to do it the other way round.

—Dr. C.R. Hallpike, *Do We Need God to be Good?*

Jordan Peterson sets these confusing word traps in a number of different ways. The upside-down pseudo-science of evolutionary psychology that he presents is one of them. For example, if a low-status ten decides to move up in the dominance hierarchy by standing up to his oppressors, and he succeeds in limiting their tyranny over him by doing so, he can expand his social territory. He rises in status, building new networks of support and success. Let us imagine that he improves himself from a ten to a seven. He is still well below the Order of the Dominance Hierarchy, but he has entered the realm of Balance, the Middle Way of the more productive order.

There are still bullies above him, but now there are also potential victims below. He could continue to stand up straight and resist his remaining oppressors, climb another rank and take more territory from his superiors. Or, if he chooses, he can begin to oppress the cowering 8s, 9s and 10s who are now below him, and rule over them as a newly acquired oppressor.

After all, does not the tyrant at the top of the hierarchy also possess good posture? Of course he does! In fact, Peterson illustrates this in great detail: the lobster at the very top of the dominance hierarchy gets everything he wants when he wants it, and he does so by standing tall and lording it over all of those beneath him.

But this tyranny of high status is a terrible thing, something Peterson very adamantly insists one should avoid practicing. After all, the Order of Tyranny relies upon creating the Chaos of the Oppressed below. In fact, the tyranny of dominance is the ultimate temptation for those on the Bottom. As the former ten continues to rise, he will naturally fantasize about rising to dominate the world, and dream of enslaving and tormenting his former bully, of giving that bully a taste of his own medicine in the Chaos of Hell.

For all that Peterson enjoys a good Disney reference, the *Cinderella* movie actually plays down this revengeful dynamic. In some older, darker versions of the tale, Cinderella not only rises out of her ash-filled

Hell to marry a prince, but her evil step-sisters' feet are mutilated in the
course of their attempts to fit into the glass slipper.

Peterson warns darkly that Chaos and Order are the two sides of a
coin. You are no better off as a tyrant than you are as the oppressed.
There is another option. The Balance. The Middle Way.

Jordan Peterson's First Rule assumes several things. First, you are an
animal. Second, in some way, large or small, you are at the bottom of
your social hierarchy or you wouldn't be reading his book. You want
to rise out of your chaotic circumstances, and Peterson wants to help
you, but only so far! As you improve your posture, as you stand up and
reject the oppression of others, you need to be careful to avoid rising
too far and run the risk of turning into a tyrant.

The Petersonian ideal is to become a balanced lobster, a middle
lobster, a productive lobster, but not a dominant one.

Peterson's first rule recognizes the reality of human social hierarchies
and on the superficial level, it is potentially useful, if prosaic, advice
for the genuinely ignorant. Standing up straight with your shoulders
back is good for your posture, both literally and metaphorically. But it
isn't the real point of the chapter. Beyond the shallow platitudes, the
deeper point of the chapter is to introduce the first of Peterson's many
paradoxes:

> *You are an animal. Dominate your environment until you achieve
> protected status in the middle of the herd. Find your place there, but
> do not go too high. Join the pack and seek the safety of anonymity in
> the middle.*

The First Principle of Jordanetics is this:
Be mediocre.

Chapter 7

The Bad Math of Balance

Did I fail any classes in university? I had to retake Stats. I wasn't good at Stats. I got it eventually... I got to be a pretty decent statistician. At least I understand the statistics now. So yeah, I didn't do very well in Statistics.

—Dr. Jordan Peterson

Rule 2: Treat yourself like someone you are responsible for helping. [Why won't you just take your damn pills?]

Taking care of yourself is an important life skill. Good sleep, a proper diet, regular exercise, and a positive internal monologue can improve your daily mood, your level of energy, and the state of your health. This is not rocket science, but it is a basic pedestrian truth that Peterson uses to deliver a deeper message that is entirely unrelated to any notion of actual self-care.

It is significant, then, that although Peterson occasionally references a few practical techniques for self-care throughout the 12 Rules for Life, he mentions precisely *none* of them while elaborating the rule that is nominally about self-care. Unless, of course, you count pharmaceuticals.

The true objective of the first rule is to position yourself safely in the middle of your social circle. The real objective for the second rule is to figure out how you are supposed to behave once you have risen out of your former status as a social reject. Combine the two objectives and it becomes clear that Jordan Peterson is offering advice on social etiquette to people who do not know how to behave in mixed company.

Why won't you take your damn pills?

Peterson begins by examining the relatively small subset of society who can best be described as non-compliant pill takers. These are people who are provided with medication, but can't be bothered to simply follow the directions and take them properly. Peterson focuses primarily on the consequences for the non-compliant individual, but it's actually a very serious matter that is threatening the effectiveness of modern medicine, as the drug-resistant mutations that result from people failing to take their full course of medication render more and more antibiotics ineffective.

Peterson admits to having marginal math skills and not infrequently demonstrates his lack of mastery of the subject. I am not familiar with the Canadian educational system, but I think it is safe to conclude that they do not teach statistics prior to the university level, since Peterson demonstrates a remarkable level of ineptitude with regards to them.

> *Imagine that a hundred people are prescribed a drug. Consider what happens next. One-third of them won't fill the prescription.*
>
> —*12 Rules for Life*

Peterson asserts that one-third of the patients studied, or 33 out of 100, were discovered to have failed to fill their prescriptions in a clinical cohort study funded by the Canadian Institutes of Health Research. But this is not true. They were not found to have done anything of the sort. What the study actually reported was that 31.3% of the 37,506 *prescriptions* written for 15,961 patients studied were not filled. Patients in different age, income, and level of physician contact cohorts had very different rates of fulfillment compliance. What this really means is that a relatively small handful of people, in most cases those with many prescriptions to fill and an assortment of other challenges, accounted for a disproportionate number of the non-filled prescriptions.

It simply isn't true that 33 percent of patients who are prescribed medication don't fill their prescriptions, let alone fail to take their pills. The study does not say that.

Overall, 31.3% of the 37,506 incident prescriptions written for the 15,961 patients were not filled. Drugs in the upper quartile of cost were least likely to be filled (odds ratio [OR], 1.11 [95% CI, 1.07 to 1.17]), as were skin agents, gastrointestinal drugs, and autonomic drugs, compared with anti-infectives. Reduced odds of nonadherence were associated with increasing patient age (OR per 10 years, 0.89 [CI, 0.85 to 0.92]), elimination of prescription copayments for low-income groups (OR, 0.37 [CI, 0.32 to 0.41]), and a greater proportion of all physician visits with the prescribing physician (OR per 0.5 increase, 0.77 [CI, 0.70 to 0.85]).

—Tamblyn

Peterson's misrepresentation of the statistics is bad enough, but he then proceeds to make another mistake, and this time it is one that cannot be blamed on his inability to understand statistics. He makes the unfounded and uncited assertion that another one-third of those hundred patients will not take their medication correctly after filling the prescription for it. The result is his groundless estimate that a mere 33 percent of all people prescribed a medication will actually take their damn pills. He doesn't just invent a statistic here, he includes it in conjunction with the first, improperly-cited statistic to reach a completely inaccurate and fictional conclusion.

Now, it is true that some prescriptions go unfulfilled and some people fail to take the medications they are prescribed even when they fill them. For example, in a study of patients suffering from schizophrenia, it was

found that 37.1 percent of them do not adhere to their advised medication regimen. That's a relatively high percentage, but Peterson's claim of
66 percent non-compliance by the general population would be nearly
twice that of schizophrenics, who are one of the most notoriously non-
compliant cohorts in the patient community, is simply bizarre.

Furthermore, surveys suggest that only about 55 percent of respon-
dents indicate that they are regularly prescribed medication in the first
place. That means that even if the general population fails to comply
with its medical regime at the same rate as schizophrenics, Peterson's
advice can only be applicable to 20.4 percent of the population. Once
again, we see Peterson's tendency to substitute a single point of evidence
for a universal principle at work. He assumes the non-compliance of his
reader in using an illustration that does not apply to more than one-fifth
of the general population.

Of course, we cannot assume that Peterson is necessarily wrong or
that Peterson's readers are a reasonable reflection of the general population. Since even the readers of a bestselling book are a very small
subset of the total population, it is not statistically impossible that
Peterson's readers are much more likely to be prescribed medication,
or fail to take it, than the average individual. And we have already seen
that Peterson's first rule is aimed specifically at society's bottom feeders.
But given Peterson's own implicit assumptions, one cannot escape the
uncomfortable conclusion that the intended core audience for *12 Rules
for Life* is comprised of social rejects too irresponsible to take the drugs
they are prescribed by their doctors.

But whoever is reading his book should not fail to notice that Peterson doesn't hesitate to compound his false assumptions and mathematical errors with further nonsense. According to him, this small group of
unwell societal losers are not responsible for their failure to follow their
doctors's orders. In fact, we are informed that clinical psychologists are
taught to assume that non-compliance is the fault of the doctor who
provides the prescription. The non-compliant patient is only refusing
medication due to a failure on the part of the prescribing physician.

We are trained to assume that the failure of patients to follow profes-
sional advice is the fault of the practitioner, not the patient. We believe
the health-care provider has a responsibility to proffer advice that will
be followed, offer interventions that will be respected, plan with the
patient or client until the desired result is achieved, and follow up to
ensure that everything is going correctly. This is just one of the many
things that make psychologists so wonderful -:).

—*12 Rules for Life*

In this passage Peterson omits key information about the nature of
the medication being described. A reader could easily assume that
Peterson is discussing general medication here, medications such as
heart pills, anti-inflammatories, and antibiotics. But he's not talking
about those medications. He's citing his training, which reflects an
intrinsically psychological perspective, and specifically refers to the
problems that many patients with mental illness have with taking their
medication.

But what is the root of those problems? Just as the lobsters were a
conceptual lead-in to the depth of the first rule, so too is the problem
with pill-taking an introduction to the secret meaning of the Second
Rule. And that hidden meaning can be traced to the connection
between shame and the supernatural origin of the cosmos.

It is of great interest, in this regard, that the five-part taijitu *(referred*
to in Chapter One and the source of the simpler yin/yang symbol)
expresses the origin of the cosmos as, first, originating in the undif-
ferentiated absolute, then dividing into yin and yang (chaos/order,
feminine/masculine), and then into the five agents (wood, fire, earth,
metal, water) and then, simply put, "the ten thousand things." The
Star of David (chaos/order, feminine/masculine) gives rise in the same
way to the four basic elements: fire, air, water and earth (out of which
everything else is built). A similar hexagram is used by the Hindus.

The downward triangle symbolizes Shakti, the femine; the upward triangle, Shiva, the masculine. The two components are known as om *and* hrm *in Sanskrit. Remarkable examples of conceptual parallelism."*

—12 Rules for Life

This is one of Jordan Peterson's more important foundational arguments: the idea that religion is a unified field. He implicitly assumes that all spiritual paths lead to enlightenment and most of the differences between individual religions are superficial. At heart, the cosmos has its supernatural origin in a single unified source, it has one ruler, one creator, and all of Man's religions ultimately agree on the identity and the purpose of that creator.

Understanding this key concept of core religious sameness is necessary in order to discover how you should act in this world. In Peterson's philosophy, Jesus Christ, is not, and cannot be, the only way to God the Father, but instead is nothing more than one of the many expressions of the cosmic truth of the Taoist Way. Like Siddhārtha Gautama or any of the subsequent bodhisattvas, Jesus Christ is merely a symbol for a man who had his Being in proper alignment through correctly following this Way of the world.

The Taoist juxtaposition of yin and yang, for example, doesn't simply portray chaos and order as the fundamental elements of Being—it also tells you how to act. The Way, the Taoist path of life, is represented by (or exists on) the border between the twin serpents. The Way is the path of proper Being.... It's the same Way as that referred to by Christ in John 14:6: I am the way, and the truth and the life. The same idea is expressed in Matthew 7:14: Because straight is the gate, and narrow is the way, which leadeth unto life, and few there be that find it.

—12 Rules for Life

As is his custom, Peterson relies upon a number of terms that he defines uniquely, and in contradiction to any of the standard dictionary meanings, while simultaneously assigning to them a deeper meaning that he seldom bothers to explain or justify. Chief among them is the term "Being" with a capital "B."

The philosopher Martin Heidigger defined Being: "that which determines entities as entities, that on the basis of which entities are already understood. . . . The Being of entities is not itself an entity."

—*Being and Time*; 26:6; translated by John Macquarie & Edward Robinson; Harper Collins, 1962

But it becomes very apparent very quickly that Peterson is not utilizing Heidigger's definition. In fact, at one point in *12 Rules for Life*, he expresses Being as a series of occupations. Lawyer, he explains, is a good game, as is plumber, physician, carpenter, or schoolteacher, because the world permits many ways of Being.

It is very clear that whatever Peterson means by "Being", it is something very different than an "ideal form" or a "determiner of entities" as defined by Heidigger. Peterson proceeds, rather unhelpfully, to try to explain his concept of Being in the negative: "The prideful, rational mind, comfortable with its certainty, enamoured of its own brilliance, is easily tempted to ignore error, and to sweep dirt under the rug. Literary existential philosophers, beginning with Søren Kierkegaard, conceived of this mode of Being as 'inauthentic.'"

From this description of an inauthentic Being, we learn that Peterson's definition of true Being is neither proud nor rational, and that an authentic mode of Being would therefore be uncertain, or at least uncomfortable with its certainty, would be humble, and irrational. True Being is neither rational nor easily tempted to ignore error.

Peterson later deigns to provide us with another clue, this time a positive one: "We share the experience of hunger, loneliness, thirst, sexual desire, aggression, fear and pain. Such things are elements of Being–primordial, axiomatic elements of Being."

So now we know that Being also has primordial elements based on needs and desires, and much later in the *12 Rules for Life*, we are informed that we ourselves possess the power to create Being out of chaos through our speech.

This would tend to suggest that chaos is neither Being nor a mode of Being. However, that conclusion directly contradicts what Peterson repeatedly tells us in earlier chapters.

- *Chaos and order are two of the most fundamental elements of lived experience–two of the most basic subdivisions of Being itself.*

- *Chaos and order are not things, or objects, and they're not experienced as such… they are perceived, experienced and understood … as personalities.*

So given these contradictions, what exactly does "Being" mean in Jordanetics? It means reaching the enlightenment of perfect Balance.

According to Peterson, Being can be bad or good, inauthentic or real, a thing or not a thing, chaos or order. And Peterson's Rules provide guidance to the reader on *all* these various modes of Being. But when you boil the concept down to its essential idea, however, Peterson points out that there is only one path to true, proper, and authentic Being, which is to maintain the Balance by following the Middle Way of mediocrity.

One hardly expects a chapter on proper care for oneself to diverge into the creation of the planet by God as outlined in the book of Genesis. But Rule 2 clearly spells out: that the psychotropic pills you are to take in order to surmount your shame is religion. But not just any religion! No, it is critical that you adhere the one, true, and authentic religion: the unified religion of Being.

It is important to emphasize here that the core of Peterson's religious perspective is that people simply don't care about themselves. They even love their pet animals more than they love themselves. He finds this situation to be intrinsically appalling.

Imagine that it isn't you who feels sick. It's your dog. So you take him to the vet. The vet gives you a prescription. What happens then? You have just as many reasons to distrust a vet as a doctor.... Thus, you care. Your actions prove it. In fact, on average, you care more. People are better at filling and properly administering prescription medication to their pets than to themselves. That's not good.... How much shame must exist, for something like that to be true?

Although it may strike you as a little ironic for a man who elevated lobsters, of all creatures, to a serve as a guide for a model of human behavior to be horrified that people might prioritize the needs of their beloved pets even to the point of self-sacrifice, it is Peterson's horror over the ethical treatment of animals that leads him to his unusual perspective on the creation of the world.

Peterson explains that as he studied Scripture, he came to understand the story of the creation of Man; Adam, Eve, the Fall from sinlessness with the help of the serpent. And, of course, while Peterson credibly claims to have studied Christianity more than he has studied any other religion, he makes a number of fundamental errors right off the bat.

He begins by claiming that the Genesis account is from two different Middle Eastern sources. But while there is an argument for the first book in the Bible being drawn from two or more sources, it is by no means a settled fact and should not have be presented as if it is. It is extremely unlikely that two entirely independent creation narratives could be so artfully woven together into a coherent, parallel, and detailed account that has made such a lasting impression on human art and spirituality, especially when there is no actual evidence suggesting this to have been the case.

Peterson's initial foray into theology quickly goes from dubious to disastrous when he introduces an argument that is as inept as it is ignorant in the very next paragraph.

Because we are so scientific now—and so determinedly materialistic—it is very difficult for us even to understand that other ways of seeing can and do exist. But those who existed during the distant time in which the foundational epics of our culture emerged were much more concerned with the actions that dictated survival (and with interpreting the world in a manner commensurate with that goal) than with anything approximating what we now understand as objective truth.... Before the dawn of the scientific worldview, reality was construed differently.

—*Maps of Meaning: The Architecture of Belief*

First, the very Holy Bible that Peterson dismisses as having been written with no concern for objective truth records the stories of individuals who quite literally question and explore the essential nature of objective truth. Second, Aristotle's *Organon* is a 3,000-page analysis of objective truth. Third, even the *Tao Te Ching*, upon which Peterson draws extensively to develop his Rules, meditates upon the nature of truth. Fourth, the skeptical school of Greek philosophy, led by the author of *Outlines of Pyrrhonism*, Sextus Empiricus, was deeply concerned with the very question which Peterson claims was not asked until some 1,700 years later!

Do you really believe that Sextus *Empiricus* was entirely unfamiliar with the concept of empirical evidence? The clue is in the name. As numerous theologians, philosophers, and historians have noted, Jordan Peterson simply does not know what he is talking about.

The basic form of reality doesn't shift from era to era. Humans don't go from breathing fire to breathing air just because Francis Bacon wrote a failed response to Aristotle in the 1500s. Reality, quite literally, is what it is, which is what it has always been. Prior to the development of modern science, humanity was not a collection of poets and dreamers trying to stay alive while operating in a mystical fog of subjective reality.

As anyone who has ever read the great Greek, Roman, or Chinese philosophers knows, as anyone who is familiar with the great Christian theologians and philosophers of the Middle Ages will recognize, it is massively false to assert that objective truth was invented circa 1518 AD or that reality was construed differently before then. This leads the critical reader to wonder, who, or what, could possibly be the source for this astonishingly incorrect claim?

Why, it is Jordan Peterson himself! The endnote on the page literally cites one J.B. Peterson.

I outlined this in some detail in Peterson, J.B. (1999). Maps of meaning: The architecture of belief. New York: Routledge.

This is a remarkable hall of mirrors that Peterson is building around himself here. He goes the New Atheists one better; whereas Richard Dawkins liked nothing better than to quote Daniel Dennett quoting Richard Dawkins, and to praise a Sam Harris book chock full of quotes from Richard Dawkins, Peterson simply cuts out the middle man and appeals to himself as the relevant authority for the nature of reality.

They don't even have a name for this logical fallacy, but they really should. Are you now beginning to understand how vitally important it is for Jordan Peterson to take his crazy pills?

And by now, it should be starting to become clear to you how Peterson carefully and cunningly twists history, religion, and the very concept of reality itself to his own ends, how he is using unobjectionable advice as bait to lead the reader down a seemingly innocuous and harmless path that does not at all lead where it appears to go.

For you see, even more integral to objective reality than matter is pain. Pain, we are informed, "matters more than matter matters." That is why, Peterson explains, so many religious traditions regard suffering to be "the irreducible truth of Being".

It also explains why pain, suffering, and shame are the core of Peterson's philosophy, as he proceeds to argue that the Biblical account of the Garden of Eden is a mythical one that explains the great behavioral mystery that has so deeply perplexed him: why people care for their pets more readily than they do for themselves.

It is due to shame, he explains, the same shame that Adam and Eve felt when they listened to the serpent, disobeyed God, and discovered that they were naked and guilty of sin. But you can almost hear the voice of that serpent whispering in Peterson's next assertion, when he declares that our fallen nature is only a problem of insufficient self-respect.

> *If we wish to take care of ourselves properly, we would have to respect ourselves—but we don't, because we are—not least in our own eyes—fallen creatures. If we lived in the Truth; if we spoke the Truth—then we could walk with God once again, and respect ourselves, and others and the world. Then we might treat ourselves like people we cared for. We might strive to set the world straight.*

> *—12 Rules for Life*

It is not an exaggeration to describe this perspective as literally Satanic, an argument that might well come out of the mouth of that devious serpent in the Garden. It is an echo of the teachings of Carl Jung, who said that the man who is at peace with himself contributes, if only in a very small way, to the good of the universe.

But Peterson goes much, much farther than Jung here. What Peterson is rejecting is the very concept of Original Sin. He is rejecting the idea that Man is intrinsically fallen, he is rejecting the idea that Man is by nature evil, indeed, he is rejecting the core Christian concept that the material world is a "silent planet" which is ruled over by the evil "prince of this world," to use the terms coined by C.S. Lewis and Jesus Christ.

You might feel guilty, sinful, and ashamed, but you will not, if only you take enough of the right sort of metaphorical pills. No wonder Peterson's insidious teachings are grasped like a lifeline by those who are drowning in the waters of their own failure, sin, and shame. He offers salvation without sacrifice, redemption without remorse.

It is also in the course of explaining the Second Rule that Peterson finally begins to define Chaos, the poison to which his rules are the antidote. He provides more than a few definitions and descriptions of it.

- The domain of ignorance

- Unexplored territory

- What extends beyond the boundaries of all states, all ideas, and all disciplines.

- The foreigner

- The stranger

- The enemy

- The rustle in the bushes in the night-time

- The monster under the bed

- The hidden anger of your mother

- The sickness of your child

- Hell

- The underworld

- The Holocaust

- A chasm

- The Abyss

He contrasts this collection of dark and scary concepts with his definitions of Order:

- Explored territory.

- The hierarchy of place, position and authority

- The structure of society.

- Tribe, religion, hearth, home and country

- The warm, secure living-room where the fireplace glows and the children play

- The flag of the nation

- The value of the currency

Monetary theory notwithstanding, Peterson's "order" is basically, on the surface, good. Chaos is basically, on the surface, bad. But, Peterson continues, "Order is sometimes tyranny and stultification, as well, when the demand for certainty and uniformity becomes too one-sided."

This is virtually identical to the nonsensical ethos to which the Force in *Star Wars* has devolved, where the Dark Side is Chaos, the Light Side is Order, and the way to goodness is not through devotion to the Light, but by keeping them in balance. In essence, what Peterson done is recreate the tedious concept of the Balance that infests so much mediocre fantasy literature today, wherein too much good is bad and too much bad is bad. This is Jedi philosophy, and not the quasi-religious Force of the first *Star Wars* trilogy. We're well into the philosophical equivalent of midichlorians here.

Trust your feelings, Jordan.

Lacking this perfect Balance, the intrinsic Chaos of our fallen nature produces the negativity that prevents us from metaphorically speaking to God, thereby causing us to suffer pain. We just have to take the damn pill, as per Peterson, but the problem for most of his readers is that none of them know what the damn pill is supposed to be!

The pill to alleviate the pain of human existence is the one true religion, and the one true religion for everyone who has learned to stand up straight and risen from the depths of the social hierarchy is the Middle Way.

Jordanetics Paradox: *The Spiritual path of The Middle Way is the only religion that works for those who have made their way to the Middle. The antidote to Chaos is not Order, it is maintaining the Balance between the two poles.*

The Second Principle of Jordanetics is this:
God is the Balance between Good and Evil.

Chapter 8

When You Need a Friend

When the structure of an institution has become corrupt—particularly according to its own principles—it is the act of a friend to criticize it.

—Dr. Jordan Peterson

Rule 3: Make Friends With People Who Want the Best for You

The Third Rule is illustrated by an unusually tragic account of one of Peterson's childhood friendships. The sensible nature of the superficial aspect of this rule, which is that you should seek friends who wish you well and will help you to raise your own standards, again has very little to do with what Peterson is describing in this chapter.

The majority of this chapter consists Peterson recounting some of his long-standing relationships with childhood friends. The relationship that features prominently throughout this chapter, and, in fact, the entire book, is a man named Chris. Chris was not only a troubled soul, whose fate still apparently haunts Peterson, but like Peterson himself, Chris represents an archetypical stand-in for humanity.

Peterson believes that Chris had an "insidious and profoundly anti-human spirit... to the serious detriment of his mental health." Chris was plagued by guilt, particularly as it related to the Native American children who also attended their school. Peterson tells us that when

Chris was attacked by those children, for whatever reason, he refused to fight back due to a belief that self-defense was not morally justifiable. He sympathized with the anger of the Native kids, and felt responsible for the fact that his white ancestors had wrongfully stolen their land, and elected to take his beatings rather than fight back.

(As an American Indian myself, let me assure the reader that while it was, indubitably, wrong for American and Canadian settlers to utilize force to settle on land that was already inhabited, and to violate treaty after treaty made with the various Indian tribes after militarily defeating them, the responsibility for these historic acts lies entirely with those who committed them, not with their descendants. Whatever anger my various Native relatives may feel about the history of the European invasion of North and Central America, and however justified that anger may be, it does not trump your individual right to self-defense.)

Chris was not the only one who refused to defend himself against the Native kids. Peterson admits that he, too, insulted a Native kid, and he, too, chose to avoid fighting. However, although Peterson literally fled from the fight, he did not do it out of any passive guilt for ancestral crimes, but out of sheer physical cowardice.

Peterson describes how his childhood friend gradually withdrew from the world as a result of his guilt. He describes how Chris developed a hatred for his own masculinity and for masculine activities. His friend somehow came to believe that obtaining an education, finding a job, or getting romantically involved with a woman was part and parcel of the ruination of the planet, and therefore to be avoided. A fascination with Buddhism helped him intellectually rationalize this ethical stance, which the observant reader will probably notice bears more than a little similarity to Peterson's own admonishment to avoid excessive Order.

Nevertheless, Peterson specifically identifies Chris as one who never adopted the Middle Way he advocates in Rule 2.

In the early 1990s, when Peterson was a new father, Chris moved in with the Peterson family, for reasons that are not given. Peterson recounts how after Chris's laziness and general negativity had caused the household tension to reach uncomfortable new heights, Peterson and his wife Tammy retreated from their own apartment on or around January 16, 1991, given some of the clues that Peterson provides in his vivid, if not entirely convincing, account.

Living with Chris was too much, Tammy said. We entered the park. The trees forked their bare branches upward through the damp grey air. A black squirrel, tail hairless from mange, gripped a leafless branch, shivered violently, struggling to hold on against the wind. What was it doing out there in the cold? Squirrels are partial hibernators. They only come out in the winter when it's warm. Then we saw another, and another, and another, and another, and another. There were squirrels all around us in the park, all partially hairless, tails and bodies alike, all windblown on their branches, all shaking and freezing in the deathly cold. No one else was around. It was impossible. It was inexplicable. It was exactly appropriate. We were on the stage of an absurdist play. It was directed by God. Tammy left soon after with our daughter for a few days elsewhere.

—12 Rules for Life

High drama or delusion? It is unclear here how the Peterson's houseguest, who could not manage to cook a meal without burning it, somehow managed to conjure a thousand demonic hairless squirrel familiars in order to provide a lifesaving warning to Tammy and the baby. As with so many of Peterson's dramatic tales, there is considerable reason to doubt his veracity, if not his sanity.

Especially since we are subsequently informed that the doomed Chris continued to live with them for nearly a year after the inexplicable flowering of frozen squirrels supernaturally warned Tammy away from the house.

Peterson has a remarkable knack for going into considerable detail with regards to even the most unlikely superficial matters, but when it comes to the more substantive elements of the situation, he paints with a vague and fact-obscuring brush. He also reveals a callous disregard for his friends' feelings; despite having earlier alienated his Native friend Rene by calling him a cow, Peterson doesn't hesitate to tell his obviously troubled best friend that he looks like a serial killer. At times, it can be difficult to ascertain precisely who is supposed to be the bad guy and who is the victim in Peterson's dysfunctional relationships.

Keep in mind that Chris was not just a poorly chosen friend who serves to illustrate the point that friends with low standards can be unhelpful to the individual who hopes to better his lot in life, Chris was a childhood friend who remained in Peterson's life for decades, sometimes on the periphery, and sometimes in the very heart of Peterson's own family.

And as Peterson describes his tragic tale, Chris spirals downward to the point that he becomes openly homicidal while staying with them. Instead of making friends who want the best for him, Peterson puts up for decades with a friend who wants to bang his wife, hates and envies his happiness, and eventually comes to wish death on him and his entire family. Of course, we can imagine that the net effect of bad friends such as Chris and Carl and Ed was a negative one on Jordan Peterson's life, but we can't possibly know what his life might been like had he more swiftly replaced these bad friends with better ones. Nor does Peterson ever speculate on the subject, or express any regret for not having followed his own advice.

This is probably because making better friends and choosing them more carefully has nothing to do with Rule 3.

In *Maps of Meaning*, Peterson writes about how, towards the end of his life, Chris wrote him a letter, in which he explained that prior to his estrangement from Peterson, they had been friends because Peterson had enough self-contempt to forgive Chris his own. But what was the difference between Peterson, upon whom fame and fortune have descended, and Chris, who died alone and penniless in a battered old pickup truck. According to Peterson, the primary difference between him and his old friends is that he was willing to improve himself by leaving them behind.

What was it that made Chris and Carl and Ed unable (or perhaps, unwilling) to move or to change their friendships and improve the circumstances of their lives? Was it inevitable—a consequence of their own limitations, nascent illnesses and traumas of the past? After all, people vary significantly, in ways that seem both structural and deterministic. People differ in intelligence, which is in large part the ability to learn and transform. People have very different personalities as well. Some are active, and some passive. Others are anxious or calm. For every individual driven to achieve, there is another who is indolent. The degree to which these differences are immutably part and parcel of someone is greater than an optimist might presume or desire. And there there is illness, mental and physical, diagnosed or invisible, further limiting or shaping our lives."

—12 Rules for Life

Peterson compares an unfortunate friend to someone who has fallen into a very deep chasm, and coldly observes that sometimes there isn't much of a body left. In other words, some friendships are not only not worth keeping, they are dangerous to the lobster who seeks to improve his status. Of course, Jordan Peterson would not be Jordan Peterson if he did not promptly proceed to argue the precise opposite of the entire argument he has hitherto presented, when he inadvertently reveals the guilt and shame he obviously feels over abandoning his childhood friends in favor of fame and fortune.

And none of this is a justification for abandoning those in real need to pursue your narrow, blind ambitions, in case it has to be said.

Do as Jordan Peterson says, gentle reader, not as he has done.

Peterson's vacillation between his ambitions and his shame over having abandoned his friends echoes the lesson of Rule 1: fight your way to the middle of the hierarchy, but no higher. However, it leaves the reader facing a difficult quandary. If you should not keep your bad friends, but you are not supposed to abandon your friends in real need, how are you to determine which friends are which? Was Chris a bad friend fallen into too deep a chasm, or was he a friend in real need whom Jordan Peterson failed to help?

Peterson looks to Jesus Christ himself to help his reader make the final determination. He observes that while Christ, being the archetypical perfect man, could afford to befriend tax collectors and prostitutes, the rest of us risk the possibility of such people bringing us down. The psychological literature, he tells us, is clear on this point: down is a lot easier than up.

Here is where Peterson provides an important warning to those are walking the 12-Rule Path: The group dynamic will affect the course of your life. It is important that you attach yourself to a successful, goal-oriented group, but it is just as important that you avoid being tainted by negative peer groups as well. Although he doesn't specifically address it in Rule 3, he emphasizes that while it is beneficial to seek out membership in a group with a positive orientation, you must do so carefully and without establishing any ideological identity with any group of people who can be collectively identified by their beliefs.

His rule ultimately means that you should never identify yourself with any specific group. Identify instead with the evolved world of enlightened individuals who aspire to universal standards for everyone. You want to avoid weak lobsters like Chris in your life, but it is up to you to determine whether they are actually low-status lobsters or fellow crustaceans of the Middle Way whose Being just happens to be out of alignment and are in need of a helping hand to restore their Balance. Unfortunately, the only way to determine whether a person in trouble is one of your fellow enlightened individuals is if you first cut them off. If you fail to feed the hungry, then one of two things will happen: they will starve or they will somehow manage to thrive on their own. If a lobster is strong enough to survive on his own, he is then worthy of your assistance and friendship.

But if not, leave them to starve and die. Success is not for the weak. Dominance is not for the lowly. That which does not kill you not only makes you stronger, it makes you worthy of friendship.

This callous Nietzschean metric is the only one provided by Peterson concerning Rule 3. The only way to determine whether your friend truly wants the best for you is to cut him out of the pack entirely. The strong dog will survive. The bad dog will wander off and die. Understanding and recognizing the difference between a bad dog and a good dog who can help you get ahead is vital for the dog who hopes to maintain his place in the middle of the pack.

Jordanetics Paradox: In the middle of the pack, it is more important to exclude the wrong friends than it is to pick the right friends. Therefore, don't hesitate to cut yourself off from any friends who might prove embarrassing or hinder your advancement.

The Third Principle of Jordanetics:
Leave the wounded behind to die.

Chapter 9

Constructing a Safe Space

What if a demon crept after you into your loneliest loneliness some day or night, and said to you: "This life, as you live it at present, and have lived it, you must live it once more, and also innumerable times; and there will be nothing new in it, but every pain and every joy and every thought and every sigh, and all the unspeakably small and great in thy life must come to you again, and all in the same series and sequence—and similarly this spider and this moonlight among the trees, and similarly this moment, and I myself.

—Friedrich Nietzsche

Rule 4: Compare yourself to who you were yesterday, not to who someone else is today

As we mature, Peterson tells us, our personal conditions become increasingly unique to us and comparisons to the lives of others become less meaningful. This is why it is necessary for us to leave the Order symbolized by our families and childhood homes and confront what he describes as "the chaos of our individual Being."

Or rather, it is normal to go off to work or to university and proceed to find ourselves, as even the most marijuana-addled stoner or dissatisfied middle-aged housewife is capable of saying much more clearly. And as we do so, Peterson warns that we must be very cautious what we might find when we finally confront that chaotic being in the metaphorical mirror, lest one become enslaved to one's own tyrannical self.

Peterson is very concerned with self-tyranny, although it is difficult to determine exactly what he means by this term. The most obvious interpretation of this notion is one's character flaws, which given Peterson's narcissism would indicate that he is referring to his own self-loathing and the self-deception with which he continues to struggle, but there are few clues in either his written works or his videos to clarify the term. It isn't really clear what sort of damage self-tyranny can inflict upon the individual so enslaved, but apparently it is serious enough that Peterson repeatedly warns against it.

One is rather tempted to conclude, as Robert Anton Wilson once said in response to Friedrich Nietzsche's self-reflective burden of eternal recurrence, that Jordan Peterson masturbates too much.

It is rather surprising to discover that Rule 4 is not about silencing your internal critic, but to the contrary, dictates listening carefully to your own voice so that you can follow its direction without becoming its obedient and harmless lap-dog. Like Virgil, the internal critic is to be a guide, to allow you to express yourself more fully and shine a light upon your inner darkness in the optimistic hope that your innermost desires might turn out to be less shameful and scary once articulated.

Peterson encourages the reader to be truthful, even to the point of danger. Doing so, he says, might reveal that in the place of your superficial, bourgeois morality, there is merely fear of your own appetites. He even suggests that perhaps telling your partner exactly what you want from them would make you more attractive as well as preventing you from being tempted by infidelity.

At this point, it's not exactly a surprise that Jordan Peterson has been accused three times of improper behavior with his students, is it? And given his penchant for autobiography as the human condition, this chapter tells the astute reader considerably more about the Peterson marriage than anyone really wants to know.

The problem with this advice to let it all hang out and let your freak flag fly should be entirely obvious. While some hidden desires are harmless enough, many of them are not. If you're dreaming about devouring your beautiful cousin or having sex with your grandmother, just to name two completely random examples for absolutely no reason at all, maybe those are dark desires that your partner and everyone else would very much appreciate if you would please keep them to yourself and your court-appointed therapist.

And this doesn't even enter into the terrible realm of violence and sex crimes that are abhorrent to every decent human being whether those desires are voiced or not. Peterson's blindness to this obvious problem is strange, considering that while he encourages the expression of hidden lusts, desires, and temptations, he also advises control of what he describes as the evil triad of arrogance, deceit, and resentment.

What is rape, incest, and cannibalism when compared to this underworld Trinity?

And yet, even these evils can serve a useful purpose. The utility of resentment, in particular, is that it reliably signifies one is experiencing excessive oppression. When you are concocting secret revenge-fantasies and experiencing "the wish to devour and destroy", that is the signal that you are free to stand up and begin exercising your lobsterial dominance without fear of becoming a tyrant.

It is at this point that the reader who is familiar with the socio-sexual hierarchy will recognize, beyond any shadow of a doubt, that *12 Rules for Life* are not actually intended to be an antidote to Chaos, they are an instruction manual for gamma males written by a confirmed gamma male. It is no wonder that the book is so popular, because it is confirming and justifying the conventional gamma instincts and delusions rather than confronting them.

For example, consider how Peterson recommends the reader talk to himself in order to take advantage of the advice of his internal critic:

> *Imagine that you are someone with whom you must negotiate. Imagine further that you are lazy, touchy, resentful and hard to get along with. With that attitude, it's not going to be easy to get you moving. You might have to use a little charm and playfulness. 'Excuse me,'" you might say to yourself, without irony or sarcasm. 'I'm trying to reduce some of the unnecessary suffering around here. I could use some help.' Keep derision at bay. 'I'm wondering if there is anything that you would be willing to do? I'd be very grateful for your service.' Ask honestly and with humility. That's no simple matter.*

> *—12 Rules for Life*

Better yet, imagine what the consequences of taking Peterson up on this advice would be! Too many conversations like this and it wouldn't be long before your friends, family, and co-workers would be looking into checking you into the local mental hospital on an involuntary basis. While modifying one's internal monologue to stress positivity instead of incessant negativity and self-criticism is known to be beneficial, Peterson isn't actually describing about normal self-talk here. He's going a step beyond that in advising his reader to enter into a state of cognitive dissociation, as if the second party to the dialogue is not the reader himself, but some kind of demon of whom the reader must be wary, and with whom the reader must negotiate.

In this chapter, Peterson talks a lot about people who are fragmented, whose shattered remnants of Being are trapped in deep chasms throughout the underworld. They are lost in hell, typically the result of having been victimized by the tyrants of Order. And yet, Peterson does not contradict Rule 3 despite the guilt he feels, and that he expects the reader to feel, when thinking of the broken people that one has left behind. Fortunately, this guilt can be alleviated by disassociating and simply refusing to think about it.

Once you notice that something bothers or concerns you, Peterson advises asking yourself three questions.

1. What is bothering me?

2. Can I fix it?

3. Am I actually willing to fix it?

And if the answer to any of those questions is no, then the reader is advised to simply ignore the nagging guilt that troubles his conscience and go in search of something to which the answer to all three questions is a positive one.

This is an insidious way to convince the reader to persistently retreat from objective reality to a subjective one. And with his advice to hyperfocus on mundane tasks that would normally require very little thought, Peterson encourages the reader to develop obsessive anxieties over things with which he cannot cope.

Maybe there is a stack of paper on your desk, and you have been avoiding it. You won't even really look at it, when you walk into your room. There are terrible things lurking there: tax forms, and bills and letters from people wanting things you aren't sure you can deliver. Notice your fear, and have some sympathy for it. Maybe there are snakes in that pile of paper. Maybe you'll get bitten. Maybe there are even hydras lurking there. You'll cut off one head, and seven more will grow. How could you possibly cope with that?

Peterson conjures imaginary serpents on every side for his reader, but instead of telling the reader how to slay them, advises that he ignore them by keeping his mind occupied with trivialities. Anyone who sincerely follows what passes for his practical advice here is almost certain to develop self-destructive habits, if not outright neuroses.

While Rule 3 begins to introduce the concept that group identity is something you should not trust, Rule 4 aims to entirely separate you from any group identities you might currently possess by encouraging you to dwell entirely inside your own mind. Don't talk to others, talk to yourself instead about various rewards you will give yourself for completing simple tasks. Don't connect to others, but disconnect from the world around you so that you can better connect to your own consciousness, your own Being.

E.M. Forster wept.

Peterson's dissociative technique relies upon taking simple, straightforward lessons and overthinking them, a process that is meant to allow the reader to graduate from a rejection of group identity to a rejection of the very heart of Western civilization. Believe it or not, Peterson very sincerely advocates a transformation of the supreme ethic of the West, which concerns the connection between Man, Creation, and the Creator, into something he describes as the positive vision of the true individual.

This is more than the expression of self-control and self-mastery, it is the admission of a fundamental desire to set the world right according to his own lights.

Ironically enough, given the fact that Jordan Peterson became famous in part due to his nominal opposition to social justice warriors, the spiritual ideal he advocates is very much in harmony with the highest abstract standard of social justice as originally defined by John Stuart Mill in 1861.

> *Society should treat all equally well who have deserved equally well of it, that is, who have deserved equally well absolutely. This is the highest abstract standard of social and distributive justice; towards which all institutions, and the efforts of all virtuous citizens should be made in the utmost degree to converge.*

> —John Stuart Mill, *Utilitarianism*

This idea of this transformative realization of the Spirit of Man is considerably more than a mere folding, spindling, and mutilating of the Christian ethic, it is an expression of something evil that is in fundamental opposition to Christianity, to the Common Law, and to the traditions of the West.

Peterson is teaching the reader that he can no longer be limited by the traditions, cultural and spiritual, of his forebears, and that even the simplest lessons from history are not to be trusted. What Peterson dictates in his Fourth Rule is for the reader to crawl so deeply inside his own self-constructed reality that he can no longer perceive the light of objective truth.

The Fourth Principle of Jordanetics:
Your head is the only truly safe space.

Chapter 10

Killing Your Inner Conan

What is best in life? To crush your enemies. See them driven before you. And to hear the lamentations of their women.

—Conan the Barbarian

Rule 5: Do not let your children do anything that makes you dislike them.

This wording of this rule is more than a little strange, and serves as a typical example of Peterson's customary bafflegarble. Could he not have simply said "Mind your kids?" Or "Spare the rod and spoil the child?" Could he not have simply flipped the double negative to a more straightforward "Teach your children to behave correctly?"

No, he couldn't. The reason is that Rule Five is not about raising your children in a way that provides them discipline, or civilizes them, or helps them become healthy and responsible adults. It is not really about raising children at all. In fact, Rule Five has nothing to do with the behavior of your children or with children in general.

Remember, Peterson's target audience are those lost Millennials who are struggling with their own identity, are very unlikely to ever marry, and are typically childless without any serious prospects for having children in the future. His secondary audience, right-of-center Baby

Boomers who find his meandering mysticism to be a comforting echo of the self-help gurus of their misspent youth, are so far past their child-rearing years that any advice to prevent children from causing their parents to dislike them is entirely inapplicable.

Besides, it's too late anyhow. Generation X has already been actively loathing the Baby Boomers for decades.

So, whatever the advice in Rule 5 concerns, it obviously isn't child-rearing. It can't be.

We know what the rule isn't, but we have yet to understand what it really is, or why Peterson chose to word it in that bizarre way. Remember, this is supposed to be one of the 12 most important rules for life! The deceptive technique that Peterson uses here has been utilized in previous rules, but it is in this chapter that he openly advocates using it as a full-blown rhetorical strategy.

What is he really advising with this rule? More importantly, as we have now learned to ask, what is the deeper message he is using the superficial one to hide?

Although in the first four rules Peterson offers advice on how to safely cut yourself off from the low-status lobsters and to dissociate yourself from any guilt you may experience as a consequence, he waits until the Fifth Rule to define what actually makes a person a lower-class lobster worthy of being excluded by the seeker of the Middle Way.

First, it is important to understand how he defines the left-behind lobsters here as he finally gives these unfortunates a name. In Rule 5, he begins to describe the example he chooses as "The God-Emperor of the Universe", which tends to strike the average user as a very strange label for what, after all, is a child ultimately doomed to low status and the oppression of Chaos as an adult.

The definitive form of the God-Emperor of the Universe is described as a little boy who once hit his daughter on the head with a toy truck, then followed up that shocking act of violence up only one year later by pushing his sister to the ground in public. This dreadful menace to society was not disciplined by his mother in either case, nor was his one-man violent crime wave brought to an end by the intervention of the police.

Peterson provides two more examples of this divinely imperial behavior, both being of very young children whose parents fail to keep them under control in public. But rather than advocating parental discipline or resorting to the humble folk-wisdom of "a stitch in time saves nine," Peterson retreats into mysticism, explaining that the incidents were classic examples of too much chaos breeding too much order as well as the inevitable reversals.

To translate that from Petersonian bafflegarble: the total lack of discipline imposed by the parents on the children permitted the children to tyrannize the parents with their bad behavior. The undisciplined child is now dominant and the situation is now one of excess Order.

Of course, the sane reader will recognize that this is not even remotely true. The child is not actually in charge. There is no excess Order, in fact, there is no order at all. It's nothing more than a common case of hapless adults proving unable to uphold their parental responsibilities.

But the significance of God-Emperors is not that they are created by bad parents who fail to discipline them. This is hardly news to anyone who has ever been a child. The real problem is that, lacking discipline as most of them do, the average Peterson reader is himself a God-Emperor. The reason why Peterson has waited to define the lower-class lobster and explain the reason for his existence until now is because it is uncomfortable to admit that we have met the enemy and they are us.

So, not only are you to be wary of the God-Emperors who may pass through your life, you are also to take measures to prevent yourself from behaving like the God-Emperor that Peterson knows you almost certainly are. Now that you have dissociated from group identity as per the Fourth Rule, you want to avoid the Triune sin of "resentment, deception, and arrogance," which leads to the evil Order of tyranny. Group identity is bad, but God-Emperor behavior is worse. If Group identity is chaos, the divine imperialism is the inevitable response of order, and the reader following the Middle Way of the 12-Rule Path must avoid both. That requires what Peterson calls discipline, which is not to be confused with the way the concept is commonly understood.

The account of the violent young truck-wielding God-Emperor is not the only time Peterson admits to having watched his handicapped daughter be abused by another child without intervening and substituting harsh, internalized judgment of the other child's parents for action, then justifying his inaction later through convoluted, abstract contemplations. He clearly has some sort of relationship with the brat's mother, and yet, as a trained clinical psychologist in witness of not one, but two, bouts of excessive violence, he has nothing to say to her, no advice to offer, and no action to take. Why not? Was he waiting to put his house in perfect order before criticizing the world? No. It is, again, personal cowardice.

Even worse, it is complete passivity in the face of the tyranny imposed by very young children.

What we see is that in the moment of conflict, Peterson doesn't hesitate to abdicate his own agency as a parental and psychological authority. He doesn't have the strength or the will to correct a small child, or even to aid the mother in correcting her child. He merely sits, watches, and silently judges, blithely ignorant of his own spectacular parenting failure.

Yet he spends most of this chapter ruminating on the very discipline he manifestly fails to impose, as a father and as a man.

Peterson's particular choice of pejorative in this chapter calls for a closer look. Of all the things he could have called the larval form of the low-status lobster, why did he choose "God-Emperor of the Universe"? Does that not strike you as a little incongruous?

In the historic sense, the idea of a man rising to demigod status, whether in ancient Rome, in ancient China or 20th-Century Japan was not considered to be a negative path. Quite the contrary, especially given the way in which divinity was usually conferred upon the Roman emperors by the Senate and their successors as a post-mortem honor.

But when we consider the wealth, power, and status that usually tends to accompany imperial divinity, if an absence of parental discipline is all that is required to transform a child into a God-Emperor of the Universe, we should all raise our children in such a lackadaisical manner.

Even the popular usages of the term are far from negative. Perhaps Peterson intended to conjure an image of the dictatorial powers wielded by the near-immortal sandworm-human hybrid God-Emperor of Arrakis, from the popular science fiction series *Dune*, written by Frank Herbert. This creature is exceedingly powerful, controls the galaxy's only supply of the anti-agathic spice, and is prone to uncontrolled bouts of lethal violence.

Another famous God-Emperor of fiction is the Emperor of Man from the *Warhammer 40k* wargaming universe, but given the fact that the Perpetual has been seated on his Golden Throne, silent and unresponsive for 10,000 years, as he empowers the psychic beacon that provides the faster-than-light Warp travel that sustains all humanity's interstellar transportation, commerce and communications, it seems unlikely that Peterson had the God-Emperor of *Warhammer* in mind.

In fact, given his familiary with Pepe, the Republic of Kekistan, and the symbolism of the American Alt-Right, we can be confident that Peterson had none other than President Donald J. Trump in mind, due to the pro-Trump meme that was originally inspired by the *Warhammer 40k* character. If you've ever seen a picture of Donald Trump wearing golden armor or bearing a gargantuan sword, then you have seen the glorious God-Emperor meme in action.

But regardless, Peterson proceeds to make it clear that the Fifth Rule does not actually concern children, but rather, the characteristics and ambitions of the adults into whom the referenced children will eventually grow.

Preferential treatment awarded a son during development might even help produce an attractive, well-rounded, confident man. This hap-

pened in the case of the father of psychoanalysis, Sigmund Freud, by
his own account: 'A man who has been the indisputable favorite of
his mother keeps for life the feeling of a conqueror, that confidence of
success that often induces real success.' Fair enough. But 'feeling of
a conqueror' can all too easily become 'actual conqueror.' Genghis
Khan's outstanding reproductive success certainly came at the cost
of any success whatsoever for others (including the dead millions of
Chinese, Persians, Russians and Hungarians). Spoiling a son might
therefore work well from the standpoint of the "selfish gene" (allow-
ing the favored child's genes to replicate themselves in innumerable
offspring), to use the evolutionary biologist Richard Dawkins' famous
expression. But it can make for a dark painful spectacle in the here
and now, and mutate into something indescribably dangerous.

—12 Rules for Life

Setting aside what we now recognize as Peterson's ignorance of evolutionary biology, the misunderstanding of the concept of the selfish
gene, and the exceedingly careless conflation of favoring a son with the
slaughtering of millions by the Mongol hordes of Genghis Khan, what
Peterson is arguing here is that a man's confidence may be good for the
individual, but represents something terrible for society.

In any event, what we are seeing here again is Peterson's fear of
excellence and his strong preference for mediocrity, couched in pseu-
doscientific moral terms.

And while we're on the subject of what Peterson assures us are his
very, very carefully chosen words, it's worth noting how often Peterson
resorts to an unusual form of phrasing in which, instead of utilizing
straightforward language, he prefers needlessly complex sentence struc-
tures. For example, when he makes a positive statement, he tends to
cloud its meaning by incorporating multiple negatives and unnecessary
perspective shifts that tend to give the careless reader the opposite
impression of what his sentence actually means.

"Do not let your children do anything that makes you dislike them" is merely the most prominent example of this tendency. In addition to the double negative "Do not/dislike," he also includes two perspective shifts. He starts with the actions of the reader, then shifts to the actions of the reader's hypothetical children then switches back to the actions of the reader.

This lack of clarity is all-too-typical of academics, of course, but the reason academics write in this manner is because they seek to avoid being easily understood! But why would anyone purposefully seek to be misunderstood in what purports to be a self-help book? Is it supposed to be a test wherein only the lobsters smart enough to solve the puzzle merit the real advice?

Or is Peterson hiding something deeper, and something darker, in plain sight?

L. Ron Hubbard, who shares much of his philosophy in common with Peterson, often made use of the same technique. Notice how Hubbard uses perspective shift and a triple negative to obscure his true intentions and true beliefs from the casual reader, while allowing those who happen to agree with his beliefs to follow the anti-Christian logic through to the end.

For a long while, some people have been cross with me for my lack of co-operation in believing in a Christian Heaven, God and Christ. I have never said I didn't disbelieve in a Big Thetan but there was certainly something very corny about Heaven et al. Now I have to apologize. There was a Heaven."

—Hubbard, L. Ron, Hubbard Communications Office
Bulletin, 11 May 1963

Such obscuration is not merely carelessness or ivory tower talk. It is an effective form of deception. It is a lie protected by shields of truth around it. And the lie that Peterson is protecting here is his true motivation, which is to explain the next step along the path of the Middle Way.

For once you have risen from the oppression of the lowly, and successfully extricated yourself from your former low-status friends, you must pass the test of the temptation that awaits you, the temptation to excel, to continue your rise, and eventually become the tyrannical God-Emperor of your Universe.

The Fifth Principle of Jordanetics:
Do not excel, because excellence endangers the Balance.

Chapter 11

The Heroism of the Couch Potato

Everyone is stupid and fooled, by me—so I can get away with whatever I want.

—Jordan Peterson

Rule 6: Set your house in perfect order before you criticize the world.

It might seem strange to those who assume Jordan Peterson is a man of the Right to discover that nearly every wall in his private residence is covered with communist propaganda from the Stalin years. Is this some sort of socialist metaphor for the perfect order that the Sixth Rule demands of the state of your own house?

Of course, Peterson isn't talking about your physical home. As we know from one of his more infamous livestream sessions, Peterson doesn't even keep his own room in order. This rule primarily concerns the challenge of cleaning up your mind and ensuring that your thoughts do not stray too far into the territory of criminal badthink such as that exhibited by the killers of Columbine High School.

Peterson observes that the Columbine killers were angered by the inequitable nature of Being and considered humanity to be contemptible and unworthy of the Earth. He describes them as the self-appointed supreme adjudicators of reality and the ultimate critics. They sought to destroy the lives of others because they saw the world as being insufficient and evil.

This take on the Columbine massacre offers an enlightening insight into Peterson's philosophy. To put it in his terms, Peterson is describing how the killers have risen from the Chaos of their low status to become God-Emperors of the tyrannical Order, only to breed more Chaos. While the killers succeeded in doing something about being oppressed bottom-feeding lobsters, they went about it the wrong way. It wasn't that they didn't rise from their lowly circumstances; they did. The problem was that they rose too fast and too far.

However, are the psychotic entries from the killers' diaries described by Peterson substantially different than his own thoughts on the world that follow?

- *"Perhaps Man is something that should never have been. Perhaps the world should even be cleansed of all human presence, so that Being and consciousness could return to the innocent brutality of the animal. I believe that the person who claims never to have wished for such a thing has neither consulted his memory nor confronted his darkest fantasies."*

- *"How can a person who is awake avoid outrage at the world?"*

- *"I had been obsessed with the idea of war for three or four years prior to that, often dreaming extremely violent dreams, centered around the theme of destruction."*

Remember, Peterson doesn't criticize the shooters for the murders they committed, but for the thoughts they were having prior to taking murderous action, thoughts that are very similar to those Peterson admits to having himself. What's more, Peterson claims that every honest person harbors violent thoughts like these!

He identifies a dualism here that divides the murderously-minded who actually commit murder from the murderously-minded who don't.

Those are the only two options, and anyone who doesn't believe himself to be obsessed with murder is delusional. Since all men are murderers in their heart, argues Peterson, the only significant distinction lies between those who put their thoughts into action and those who don't.

In other words, both chaos and order are to be found in action whereas more perfect order requires non-action.

So, what, exactly is the difference between Peterson's world-killing fantasies, and the murderous fantasies of the low-status lobsters who rose up to become God-Emperor tyrants with guns and brought their fantasies to life? How do you choose to become the correct sort of violent fantasist whose life will not result in harming and even murdering others?

By putting your house in order, we are told. By ordering your own experience.

If Peterson is to be believed, the Columbine killers' real crime was not that they possessed the courage of their evil and violent convictions, but that they failed to deal successfully with the bullies inside their own minds. They did not put their own house in order, but made the mistake of responding to real-world problems in a real-world manner.

Rule 6 presents a new practice in the Middle Way that is nevertheless consistent with the previous rules: the correct response to oppression is to do nothing. This is not a new concept, but it is a largely foreign one to Western philosophy. *Wu wei*, the Chinese philosophers call it, the action of non-action.

> *When man is born, he is tender and weak;*
>   *at death, he is hard and stiff.*
> *When the things and plants are alive, they are soft and supple;*
>   *when they are dead, they are brittle and dry.*
> *Therefore hardness and stiffness are the companions of death,*
> *And softness and gentleness are the companions of life.*
> *Therefore when an army is headstrong, it will lose in a battle.*

When a tree is hard, it will be cut down.
The big and strong belong underneath.
The gentle and weak belong at the top.

—Lao Tzu, *Tao Te Ching*

Retroactively justifying his hapless passivity when confronted by children bullying his daughter, as well as his failure to help the woman raped by Schroedinger, Peterson discovers virtue in his commitment to non-action. Stop paying attention to politics, or the injustices perpetrated by your enemies, he urges his readers. Because you are not perfect, you have no right to compete for a better place in the hierarchy, much less attempting to tear down and replace the entire infrastructure. By mentally checking out in this way and withdrawing into the safe space of your imagination, you can express your virtuous dismay and dissatisfaction with the unsatisfactory reality of the world without harming it, or changing it, or even interacting with it.

Peterson posits that if only everyone would do nothing, the world would cease to be an evil place. And with continued non-effort, the collective Spirit of Man might even be able to bring about an end to tragedy and create paradise right here on Planet Earth.

In Peterson's philosophy, the world is fallen into evil due to the actions of men. If men acted benevolently by staying inside their own heads and limiting their actions to their imaginations, Paradise on Earth would be the result. It is hard not to notice the overt parallels to Aleister Crowley's Satanic philosophy. Like Peterson, Aleister Crowley also believed that Heaven could be constructed on Earth, but only if enough men managed to master themselves.

Every man must overcome his own obstacles, expose his own illusions.

—*Liber Causae*

Crowley and Peterson both agree that Heaven on Earth awaits the man who wills to make it manifest in his own life. And Peterson's imperative of having everything in perfect order is also deeply connected to Crowleyan mysticism.

Know firmly, o my son, that the true Will cannot err; for this thine appointed course in Heaven, in whose order is Perfection.

—*Liber Aleph*

The primary difference between Peterson and Crowley is that Peterson does not delve into the obvious implications of this belief in creating Heaven on Earth quite as extensively as Crowley. Crowley argues that, as bad as the Earth can be, it is not a prison or a permanent hell, but rather a temple to the sacrament of life, where the essence of everything is played out. This is why acting on the basis of your judgment of the world is a bad idea. Attacking the world, even if it appears to be worthy of destruction to you, is an attack on the temple and the intrinsic joy of life.

Ironically, Peterson's perspective is even darker than that of the notorious "Beast 666", for Peterson cannot even conceive of the joy of life in a world of suffering and pain. And while Peterson's defenders will undoubtedly be tempted to question the connection between Peterson's philosophy with the Thelemite beliefs of the infamous sex magickian and master of the Ordo Templar Orientis, or with the controversial founder of the Church of Scientology, L. Ron Hubbard, the spiritual connections are undeniable.

One merely has to review Hubbard's Eight Dynamics of Scientology to see the obvious synchronicity between them and Peterson's twelve rules. Symbolized by the octodirectional cross of Scientology, the Eight Dynamics provide the practicing Scientologist a guiding framework for life. And as with Jordanetics, survival is the core foundation of Hubbard's Dianetics.

Eight Dynamics	Twelve Rules
1. Self	1. Stand Up Straight
	2. Treat Yourself Like Someone You Are
	4. Compare Yourself to who you were yesterday
2. Sex/Children	5. Do not let your children do anything...
3. Group	3. Make friends with people who want the best for you
	11. Do not bother children when they are skateboarding
4. Mankind	6. Set Your House In Perfect Order Before You Criticize the World
	9. Assume that the Person You Are Listening To Knows Something that You Don't
5. Life Forms	12. Pet A Cat When You Encounter One On The Street
6. Physical Universe	8. Tell the Truth—or At Least Don't Lie
7. Spirit	7. Pursue What is Meaningful
8. Infinity	10. Be Precise in Your Speech

It is important to remember that, unlike the Eight Dynamics of Scientology, the 12 Rules of Jordan Peterson are not literal. It isn't until you study the written meanings of the rules that you can begin to make sense of the coded rule titles. For example, if you were to make the mistake of going by the title of Rule 8: Tell the Truth—or At Least Don't Lie, it would be easy to assume it has nothing to do with the Physical Universe, or man's place in it. To the contrary, Peterson's

Rule 8 corresponds directly to the Sixth Dynamic of Scientology as it concerns the occult principle of using one's thoughts and speech to make manifest the physical world around the speaker.

In the same way, the Sixth Rule is not about literally vacuuming the carpets and dusting the bookshelves, but concerns curbing your negative impact on the world by focusing on an interior struggle rather than an external one. Even though the world is fallen, you cannot hate or judge the world in its own right. The world is you, you are the world, the two are inseparable, and the world's improvement can only begin to take place inside your own head.

We aren't talking about simply avoiding shooting up a school here. Peterson wants you to avoid bringing the uncleanliness of chaos to the global setting. You must first work out your own issues, and do it slowly. If you can achieve that, and everyone else does the same, a better world can be created. So don't criticize the world and ruin it for the rest of us.

Of course, even on the practical level, the advice given in the Sixth Rule is a complete non-starter. How can you possibly focus on putting your bedroom in order when the barbarians have broken down the front door, forced their way into the kitchen, and are cheerfully smashing all the dishes?

The Sixth Principle of Jordanetics:
Inaction is always preferable to action.

Chapter 12

The Self-Crucifixion of the Crazy Christ

You can choose a ready guide in some celestial voice.
If you choose not to decide, you still have made a choice.

—Rush, "Free Will"

Rule 7: Pursue What is Meaningful (Not What is Expedient)

For something that is seldom billed as either philosophy or spiritualism, Jordanetics often tends to strike a highly religious note. Fans of Jordan Peterson often speak of him in awed, reverential tones, and he has observably attracted a devout following that can only be described as cult-like. Although he utilizes a wide variety of religious allusions and illustrations throughout his first six rules, it is not until the introduction of the Seventh Rule that he begins to openly address a religious imperative.

He describes an ominous vision of flying, during which he soared over a tremendous landscape that was filled to the horizon with massive glass pyramids that were full of people trying to climb to the top of them. And above each pyramid was a Sauron-like disembodied eye that simultaneously transcended and watched over the frantic activity below in a patient, predatory manner.

The occultic symbolism of Peterson's vision is not particularly difficult to recognize. This is imagery often mentioned in reference to the Osiris/Horus/Christ melange to which he frequently refers. The pyramids are Egyptian, the bird's-eye view is an oblique reference to the All-Seeing Eye of Horus, usually represented by an owl with one eye. Peterson, in the vision, is transcending the world below like the illuminated elite he serves. In his vision, he is beyond Heaven, beyond Hell, and beyond the chaos of the world, soaring free in glorious and unfettered detachment.

Carl Jung, who serves as a sort of John the Baptist to Jordan Peterson's Christ, once wondered what preceded the Osiris myth, which can be traced back about 6,000 years. But Jung, like Peterson, is convinced that the Osiris legend was the seed of what both men consider to be the Jesus myth, although Peterson always does his best to avoid being forced to directly answer the question, even when specifically pressed to do so.

The Sixth Rule is intended to guide you as you venture out from your spotless house, ready to enter into engagement with the world without judging it. Peterson's vision provides his credentials; like the floating eyes, he is above the fray and is therefore more than capable of guiding you through the chaotic circles of the World-Hell, a Virgil to your Dante, permitting you to enter the world without attempting to enslave it, and enabling you to eventually be transformed into a floating detached eye yourself.

The pursuit of meaning to which Peterson provides the map necessarily involves transition, not just from low-status lobster to the Middle Way, but from man to demigod. At the beginning of the chapter, Peterson identifies the transition of men from animal to human. While he admits, for once, that his account is nonsense from a scientific perspective, he deems it sufficiently correct thematically to serve as a useful analogy.

In this developmental progression, men learn the art of longer time preferences through the killing of large animals that provide too much meat to be devoured immediately. From these longer time preferences, man develops the ability to distinguish between mammoth-now and mammoth-future, which inevitably led to the development of various concepts such as sacrifice, personal reputation, the social contract, compound interest, and the Black-Scholes formula for the pricing of options and corporate liabilities.

All right, I must confess that I added the last two items on the list, but I hasten to point out that they only make Peterson's anthropological invention funnier, they don't actually render it any more ridiculous than it already was. So, as we so often must do with Peterson's fanciful excursions into the past in order to explain the present, we must set aside both actual history and science in an attempt to discern his actual purpose.

The Seventh Rule therefore concerns the socio-spiritual course an individual is advised to take once he has found his place in the middle of the pack, ditched his former friends, and avoided the temptation of lording it over others. But the path Peterson is encouraging the reader to walk is a winding and serpentine one.

Rather fittingly, concerning his own habitual dishonesty and the deceptive nature of his books, Peterson makes frequent reference to snakes, the very worst of which he tells us is the eternal human proclivity for psychological, spiritual, personal, and internal evil. But if this excursion into metaphor is not surprising, Peterson soon reverts to his customary incoherence when he suddenly shifts his focus back to his very poor grasp of biological science and wonders if human vision was an evolutionary adaptation that resulted from the necessity of detecting snakes, then theorizes that this nonexistent adaptation might explain the way in which the Virgin Mary was often depicted in medieval and Renaissance art.

This stream of incoherence goes well beyond simple ignorance, as the following observations will suffice to demonstrate.

First, human vision is neither stunningly acute nor is it unique. Both birds of prey and sharks have better vision than humans, while horses and other herd animals have nearly 360 degree vision as well as better night vision. Bees see more colors and cats require less than one-sixth the amount of light that humans do.

Second, given that every year ten times more people die from lightning strikes than from snake bites, it is less likely that human evolution has been affected by poisonous snakes in any way, shape, or form than by a single talking snake in the Garden of Eden. Despite his profession of a dedication to the Darwinian truth, Jordan Peterson clearly does not understand how the theory of evolution is supposed to work. Even if we posit an ancient population bottleneck, the number of historical snake bite deaths required to make a snake-spotting mutation a reproductive advantage to *Homo sapiens sapiens* is several orders of magnitude higher than is conceivable to any sane biologist or statistician.

Third, the fact that the Virgin Mary is keeping her infant well away from the poisonous snake has absolutely nothing to do with her keenly evolved snake-spotting vision, it is simply an artistic combination of a mother defending her child incorporating a visual reference to a well-known Bible verse.

Following an equally bizarre exploration of fruit and color, Peterson declares that this dread snake, this symbol of chaos, this embodiment of evil, also gives men great mystical visions and dreams, as per the endowment of the knowledge of good and evil upon humanity in the Garden of Eden.

With all the discussion of Jesus and Mary and Adam and Eve, it should be no surprise to discover that this rule concerns a decidedly religious course of inquiry. If you have followed the Rules to this point, you have begun to rise through the social order. You have begun to sort out the material world along the way, and in doing so, you have risen above the underworld of the oppressed.

Continuing with the Genesis theme, Peterson returns to Cain as a symbol of chaos. But incredibly, he claims that the story of Cain is an abstract precursor of Jesus Christ's sojourn in the wilderness. Here

Peterson comes to what may be his ultimate statement on religion, and its central importance to the Seventh Rule.

> *'No tree can grow to Heaven,' adds the ever-terrifying Carl Gustav Jung, psychoanalyst extraordinaire, 'unless its roots reach down to Hell.' Such a statement should give everyone who encounters it pause. There was no possibility for movement upward, in that great psychiatrist's deeply considered opinion, without a corresponding move down. It is for this reason that enlightenment is so rare.*
>
> —*12 Rules for Life*

Peterson underlines the point by utilizing this concept to explain his deep mystical understanding of Christ's desert encounter with the Devil and his subsequent taking the sins of the world onto himself and accepting the responsibility of paying for them. Far from being a sinless scapegoat for mankind, Peterson's Christ is a Crowleyesque all-sinner, to whom nothing human is alien and no sinful act is unknown.

This idea of Jung's, which Peterson finds so deeply informative with regards to the observed scarcity of enlightenment, is similar to that of the occultist's *Emerald Tablet*, upon which is inscribed:

> *As Above, so Below, and as Below, so Above, in the Accomplishment of the Miracle of the One Thing.*
> *And just as all things have come from One, through the Mediation of One, so all things follow from this One Thing in the same Way."*

In fact, Carl Jung himself found deep and direct inspiration from the *Emerald Tablet*, relying on his own dream interpretation of a green stone tablet that appeared to him in a series of visions. This informed his writing of the private hermetic work, *Seven Sermons to the Dead*. Jung's "branches of heaven" are "As Above" and the roots are "So Below."

Aleister Crowley explained the operations of the *Emerald Tablet* in similar terms.

That is to say, in order to perform his miracle, [the Magician] must call forth his own God in the Microcosm. That is united with the God of the Macrocosm by its likeness to it; and the Macrocosmic force then operates in the Universe without as the Magician has made it operate within himself; the miracle happens. And as the macrocosm is the greater, it follows that what one does by magick is to attune oneself with the Infinite.

—*The Revival of Magick*, 1917

So, Peterson's philosophy is significantly influenced by this esoteric tradition, in which the cause from above is directly reflective of the effect below and vice versa; the causes from below have effects that resonate through the cosmos. Too much order leads to too much chaos. As Above, So Below. You've got to go through Hell before you get to Heaven.

Of course, this philosophy can hardly be considered particularly profound, as it has been expressed many times in many ways, including the song "Jet Airliner" by the Steve Miller Band.

The esotericism of Jung and Crowley and Hubbard also influences Peterson's 12-Rule Path with regards to the state he describes as Being. Being means that "Christ is forever He who determines to take personal responsibility for the full depth of human depravity." Here Peterson's "He" does not refer to the historical figure of Jesus Christ of Nazareth. What Peterson is saying is that anyone who takes "personal responsibility for the full depth of human depravity" is a Christ. As a psychologist who has dedicated himself so profoundly to the Holocaust and to the Hell of human existence, there would be little doubt that Peterson sees himself as one of these Christs following Jung's roots into darkness even if we did not possess documentary evidence of Peterson's Messiah complex.

Christ the symbol rejects the dominance hierarchy, as does Peterson the Self-Perceived Messiah, in order to save the world from itself.

I came to believe that survival itself, and more, depended upon a solution to the problem of war.... I had a notion that confronting what terrified me—what turned my dreams against me—could help me withstand that terrible thing. This idea—granted me by the grace of God—allowed me to believe that I could find what I most wanted (if I could tolerate the truth; if I was willing to follow wherever it led me; if I was willing to devote my life to acting upon what I had discovered, whatever that might be, without reservation—knowing somehow that once started, an aborted attempt would destroy at least my self-respect, at most my sanity and desire to live).

—*Maps of Meaning: The Architecture of Belief*

The letter to his father quoted in *Maps of Meaning* is the key to understanding absolutely everything you need to know about Jordan Peterson and his philosophy. Combined with the evidence provided by the *12 Rules for Life*, the inescapable conclusion is that Jordan Peterson is a mentally ill occultist who seeks to save the world from nuclear destruction by uniting the nations of Man under a single global government through a collective devotion to his esoteric religious philosophy.

More than one hundred years ago, Carl Jung suffered a profound and disturbing experience he called his confrontation with the unconscious. What we might describe as a midlife crisis today, given that he was approaching 40 at the time, he himself described as being menaced by a psychosis, while at other times he believed himself to be caught up in the throes of schizophrenia. Like Peterson, he saw visions and heard voices. He began inducing hallucinations through drugs and meditation, and recorded his experiences in illuminated script and paintings and notes in a large red leather-bound book which he called the *Liber Novus*, or more casually, the *Red Book*. He secretly added to the book for more than 16 years. Over the course of the next 80 years it was read by fewer than two dozen people, until, about ten years ago, the Jung estate finally permitted the publication of the book.

In concert with the origins of the *Red Book*, Carl Jung and a few friends founded a group called Psychological Club in 1916. It continues, to this day, as a gathering of leading doctors, attorneys and scientists, to study Jung's analytical psychology. It is remarkable to read a description of one of these seminars, as one could readily believe that it is Peterson, not Jung, being described in these weighty terms.

> *An involuntary hush falls on the room as Jung himself stands quiet and grave for a moment, looking down at his manuscript as a sailor might look at his compass, relating it to the psychological winds and waves whose impact he has felt on his passage from the door. The hush in the assembly means not only reverence but intense expectation. What word adventure shall we have today with this creative thinker? What question, like the stroke of a bronze bell, will he leave ringing in our minds? What drastic vision of our age will he give us that will help us to lose our sense of problems, subjective and oppressive, and move into a more universal and objective realm?*

—Elizabeth Shepley Sergeant, *Harper's*, May 1931

Like Jung, Peterson portrays Christ as one of the avatars of a symbolic person, an Everyman who has appeared in many concepts throughout the ages. Christ is merely one form among many. What Christ, and the All-seeing Eye, and Marduk and the Logos all represent is the expression of Being as Peterson defines it. This identification of Jesus Christ as the All-Seeing Eye is a particularly important one that is significant in the analysis of the later rules.

Although Peterson frequently refers to the Logos, he never defines it very specifically. Jung did in a 1934 interview called C.G. Jung Speaks: "Christ the LOGOS—that is to say, the mind, the understanding, shining into the darkness. Christ was a new truth about man. Mankind has no existence." Peterson does, however quite literally, compare himself to Christ.

- "Christ takes a different path. His sojourn in the desert is the dark night of the soul"

- "It drove me into the desert, into the long night of the human soul."

Peterson's Christ complex is too obvious to miss, but what might be easy to overlook is his declared confusion over his inability to comprehend the Cold War. It was during his time in the desert that he found himself walking the enlightened Middle Way between the the U.S.A. and the Soviet Union, two great armed factions with missiles aimed at each other. It is here that we finally begin to comprehend why Peterson has filled his family home with the chaotic Hell of Soviet propaganda, as opposed to the ordered Heaven of American propaganda. The two factions are the two halves of the Taoist duality, the twin serpents of the yin-yang.

Peterson, in portraying himself as a visionary Christ-figure capable of saving Man from material destruction, is personally demonstrating his philosophy in action. Just as one must rise to the middle of the Pack in order to escape the chaos of the bottom of the Dominance Hierarchy, one must rise through the ranks of Hell to work one's way into Heaven. The only path to true enlightenment is the one that he has found, acting wisely through inaction while making the decisive choice not to choose.

Although Peterson never openly states that the Resurrection of Jesus Christ never happened or that Christianity is merely a symbolic religion rather than a true reflection of the spiritual world, he makes it clear that despite the esoteric power its symbolism represents, the Christian faith itself is baseless and its moral tradition is of little more than historic utility. He compliments the faith but in an abstract way, referring to it in the past tense, as if it has already fulfilled its ultimate purpose in laying the groundwork for the next step in religion that Jordanetics represents.

This is not to say that Christianity, even its incompletely realized form, was a failure. Quite the contrary: Christianity achieved the well-

nigh impossible. The Christian doctrine elevated the individual soul,
placing slave and master and commoner and nobleman alike on the
same metaphysical footing, rendering them equal before God and the
law.

—12 Rules for Life

While Christianity did help Man progress further along the path of true religion, Peterson deems it to now be obsolete. There is a transcendental next step that awaits the Spirit of Man, a transcendence to a state beyond the good and evil of Christianity. If the worldview of Jordanetics is correct, Man began as a mere beast at the time of his creation, worshipping the confusing forces around him, before he gradually evolved, mentally and spiritually. One of those evolutionary developments was Christianity, upon which additional advancements have been made. But as Christianity and its various fruits, including science and modern progressive morality, imposed excessive Order by solving many problems that were previously insoluble, this created a need for something more suited to address the ever-mutating Chaos of Being.

The antidote of Chaos is not Order; it is the transcendent religion of the Balance, a religion in which Heaven cannot be gained without first experiencing in full the emptiness of the wilderness and the agonies of Hell. Peterson, by his own admission, has become the Christ of this new religion, because he has paid, and continues to pay, the price in the coin of human suffering.

If you hope to follow his example and achieve similar enlightenment, you too, must pay the price demanded by Rule 7. You must descend into your personal Hell and suffer upon your own Cross before you can be resurrected into enlightenment.

The Seventh Principle of Jordanetics:
To reach Heaven above, you must descend into Hell below.

Chapter 13

A Glib and Forked Tongue

I won't denounce my previous self.

—Dr. Jordan Peterson

Rule 8: Tell the Truth—Or, At Least, Don't Lie

After you descend into Hell, you must learn to navigate its Chaos. But while the oppressive language of Order is truth, the language of Chaos is the lie.

Peterson openly admits his propensity to lie. He is, in fact, a deeply practiced and natural liar, who admits, "I soon came to realize that almost everything I said was untrue." This tendency affords him the ability to navigate and express the language of Hell.

Since the true religion is an esoteric Jungian form of enlightenment, one of the first expressions of that practice is through one's speech. A creed is expressed, after all, using words. The Eighth Rule provides the newly enlightened maintainer of the Balance a means of training for his speech. It also pulls the curtain back on the techniques Peterson customarily uses to communicate his teachings. It is also in this chapter that he reveals a considerable amount of useful information about his own interior world.

Recall here that Hell is a necessary component of Peterson's religious approach towards bringing Heaven to Earth. Contemplating Hell fully and deeply is the only correct way to navigate the microcosm of the Below here and now in order to achieve the infinite heaven of the cosmic Above. This is why Peterson so obsessively returns to the horrors of the Holocaust and the totalitarian chaos of Stalinism. In his experience, these are the accessible expressions of Hell, which provide him with the paths that will eventually lead to enlightenment.

In his own convoluted way, Peterson has addressed the nature of God through his comparisons of himself with the Christ, who is the avatar of God. He has also advocated various elements of Taoism, and references various aspects of Thelemism as well, but as a gnostic, he never openly expresses a coherent religious creed. This is another indicator of his habitual disinclination to tell the truth, because creeds and doctrine are how religions articulate and define their perceptions of truth.

Peterson approaches the question of what truth is from an unusual angle. Instead of defining truth as a category, and revealing what he believes to be contained in it, he begins by first defining lies.

Even more strangely, Peterson begins *by lying about lying!*

He first quotes *Mein Kampf* in order to assert that Hitler clearly stated "you need the lie". But the portion he quotes is actually Hitler's *critique* of the Big Lie, the idea that people are much more likely to fall for a ridiculous lie of colossal proportions rather than a small and plausible one. Read that last sentence again. Peterson is literally redefining the concept of criticism as advocacy! Hitler was a confirmed *critic* of this deceptive rhetorical technique, not a proponent!

Hitler attributed the Big Lie to his enemies, capitalists and Jews, while Goebbels later declared the English utilized it. But Peterson, in his quest to identify the totalitarian mindset as something beyond ordinary evil, portrays Hitler as openly endorsing this form of shameless lying, rather than as criticizing it. This is, of course, not the first time in the book that Peterson has dared to blatantly misrepresent the words of others, but it is the first time he has done so with the words of someone whose ideas are so well known and so easily checked.

Why on Earth would Peterson lie about Hitler's own words and exaggerate them? Why would anyone ever feel the need to do so? Were Hitler's actual words and deeds really not evil enough in themselves?

Now if you are insufficiently familiar with Peterson's work, you might be tempted to try to defend him by arguing that because Hitler was aware of the utility of the Big Lie in the hands of his enemies, he eventually adopted the practice itself. But that is not a viable defense, because Peterson was quoting *Mein Kampf* in order to demonstrate that Hitler's objective was to create Hell on Earth and to generate Chaos by telling Big Lies. This is completely untrue and is not supported in any way by the text. Furthermore, although he quotes Hitler's definition of the Big Lie and adopts the concept as his basis for the unique relationship between tyranny and the establishment of Hell on Earth, Peterson immediately proceeds to contradict the very definition he just cited.

According to Hitler, the insidious Big Lie works on the masses because the average individual can't conceive of trying to get away with telling blatant lies. The Big Lie works because one bypasses the little lies to which the average individual is attuned and tell massive whoppers that are so obviously untrue that one would almost have to be a complete lunatic to tell it with a straight face.

But Peterson contradicts the concept right after quoting Hitler's explanation of it. Instead, he claims instead that you first need to tell the little lies in order to tell the big lie.

Why is this error important? Because it totally undermines the superficial level of the Eighth Rule, which states that one can transform the world simply by telling the truth, or at least not telling lies. And it should cause even the most enthusiastic Peterson fan to wonder why Peterson would so shamelessly misrepresent something so easily checked by a simple recourse to Wikipedia.

One might even go so far as say that Peterson tells a Big Lie about the nature of the Big Lie.

One of the more alarming aspects of Jordanetics is the innovative approach to deception it offers. Other religions make allowances for deception under certain circumstances. Both Islam and Judaism are religions that provide specific allowances for lying to outsiders in certain specific situations. When these exceptions are applied, in addition to sparing an adherent from persecution, this principle of "faithful deception" or "lying for higher purposes" has a universal, strategic utility.

While Nathan Hale may be revered as the American Revolutionary whose famous last words at age 21 were "My only regret is that I have but one life to give for my country," he was only caught because he wasn't a very good liar. Far more adept in his spycraft was James Armistead Lafayette, a slave who was such an effective double-agent that he was maintained on both the British and the American payrolls during the Revolutionary War. So, there are reasonable arguments to support ethical deception, but these arguments are always exceptions to the rules that dictate honesty.

To the contrary, the 12-Rule Path doesn't merely allow for lying out of necessity, or under certain well-defined parameters. The Jordanetics imperative is to proactively deceive and to strive to avoid saying anything that can be readily compared to the objective truth.

The point is that Peterson isn't actually telling you not to lie with this rule. In fact, he's lying about lying. If he's serving as a double agent here, he's not working for you, even though you may have paid for his book. Who, then, is he serving?

Armistead, a slave working for the American revolutionaries, pretended to have escaped his master and fled to the British in order to ingratiate himself with them. The British paid him to spy on the Americans. He returned to the Americans and obtained false documents from them regarding their troop numbers and movements which he then smuggled back to the British in order to mislead their intelligence.

Peterson's confessions of his past dishonesties is meant to deceive you into believing that Peterson is now a reformed liar. He tells you the misleading truth about his past lies, implying that he is now unusually honest and upright because he struggled like Hercules against his vast inner world of lies and self-deceptions. But in his most recent book, we've seen him lie about everything from small towns and statistics to Hitler. His lies are told relentlessly, perhaps even pathologically, and yet he expects you to accept his guidance when he finally reveals his deceitful approach toward telling the truth.

He claims to have cleansed his personal house of all deception and iniquity by very, very carefully choosing his words, deeply contemplating the various pros and cons of each and every measure, and painstakingly weighing the truth. But this is a false pose, just as his pretense to be carefully considering every question he is asked on stage as if it was the first time he had ever encountered it is an act.

Because Peterson equates truth with survival, or rather, anything that increases one's chances of survival, truth is intrinsically subjective. And since there is no such thing as objective truth, the only thing you can do to be truthful, by which he means increase your chances of survival, is to is master the art of the lie. Peterson is qualified to teach you this rule because he has, by nature and philosophy, become a spiritual master of lies. Peterson lies regularly and habitually, and here he presents a rule that does not only allow for lying under limited circumstances, but presents dishonesty as a fundamental ethic.

He is not only willing to misrepresent Hitler, he is just as willing to misrepresent Jesus Christ. He writes, "In His human form, Christ sacrificed himself voluntarily to the truth, to the good, to God. In consequence, he died and was reborn." This is not accurate Christian theology. Jesus Christ did not sacrifice himself to the truth and the good, but to liars and deceivers, to a corrupt system of religion and careless system of government. In consequence, he died and, depending upon whom you ask, either remained in the grave or rose from the dead.

No one, Christian or not, claims that Jesus Christ was reborn. It is the Christian believer who must be born again, not Christ.

He continues his assault on basic Christian theology with an even more blatant lie: "The Word that produces order from Chaos sacrifices everything, even itself, to God. That single sentence, wise beyond comprehension, sums up Christianity."

It is important here to note for the non-Christian reader that the first sentence in the above quote is original to Jordan Peterson. It is not to be found anywhere in the Bible or in the writings of any Christian theologian. Thus, when he describes the sentence as being wise beyond comprehension, Peterson is narcissistically praising himself and what passes for his own wisdom. That single sentence is neither wise nor accurate. Any summation of Christianity that excludes the fallen nature of Man is not correct. To leave out the Fall, the Cross, and the Resurrection is to entirely miss the point of Christianity.

It is not an accident that Peterson became famous through videos and lectures rather than his writing. He is a performer. He simultaneously combines an image of personal vulnerability with a commanding stage presence. He has a melancholy charisma and generates audience sympathy through his emotions. He'll cry. He'll rant. He'll fall into sudden silences, glare balefully into the camera, or wag a finger at the audience. He'll draw upon his outdated, rustic colloquialisms ("Bucko") and hypnotically enspell his viewers with his disarming, soft-spoken Canadian accent.

Not since Adolf Hitler has there been a more artfully practiced public speaker. It would not be at all surprising if a video archive of Peterson practicing his gestures and expressions in the mirror were discovered in the future.

None of performance art comes through in his writing, nor is it capable of disguising the actual content. *12 Rules for Life* is a meandering and deceptive work, and *Maps of Meaning* is an incredibly tedious stream of incoherent citations. While his thoughtful posturing and folksy digressions may be engaging in public presentations, in print, they serve only to infuriate the logical reader.

Part of this is because Jordanetics, at its heart, is about keeping secrets. Peterson doesn't actually want most of his readers to correctly understand his psycho-religious knowledge. Its a hard-won, thing, you see. It isn't for everyone. Like all secret wisdom, it is only for the elite. Most of you can't see the truth, you can't handle the truth, and you are therefore unworthy of it. Peterson's fog of meaning, to which he provides the map, ensures that only the most persistent individual, willing to go brave the Hell of Enlightenment and able to endure the Underworld of suffering, pain, and Chaos can begin to master his higher truths. But, by his own declaration, most of his readers are lowly denizens of Hell, unable to rise out of their oppression, and only useful to him in providing money, a fan base, and object lessons.

Part of this is because watching an expressive, emotive actor brood about lobsters while pretending he understands science is something some people happen to find entertaining. But the thoughts of an actor, whether it is Jordan Peterson doing his deep and careful thinker routine on stage or Bill Nye the Science Guy, are seldom very intelligent or interesting. One of Peterson's strengths is that he doesn't sound like an academic when he lectures. The subject matters he addresses are often shallow things such as Disney movies, mean girls, what he eats, the suicidal behaviors of his crazy friends, and the stupid things he did when he was a child. But this anti-academic style doesn't work very well in a book filled with hundreds of citations, and the fact that so many of the citations are misleading, misinterpreted, or irrelevant renders the book even less convincing to the intelligent, well-educated reader.

12 Rules for Life is not a subversion or a critique of academia, as some would have it. It is an esoteric religious pamphlet published in pseudo-academic self-help wrapper.

But you need not take my word for Jordan Peterson's dishonesty. He was quite willing to share his Clintonian approach to the truth in his debate with Sam Harris, a debate so disastrous that he concocted one of his most jaw-droppingly absurd lies yet in order to try to explain away what amounted to an exercise in intellectual self-humiliation.

Harris: "You clearly have to have a conception of facts and truth, that is possible to know, that exceeds what anyone currently knows

*and exceeds any concern about whether it is useful or compatible with
your own survival even to know these truths."*

*Peterson: "Well then I would say that I don't think that facts are
necessarily true. So I don't think that scientific facts—even if they
are correct from within the domain that they were generated—I don't
think that that necessarily makes them true..."*

*Harris: "The truth value of a proposition can be evaluated whether
or not this is a fact worth knowing or whether or not it's dangerous to
know."*

*Peterson: "No, but that's the thing I don't agree with because I think
that's the kind of conception of what constitutes a fact that does in
fact present a moral danger to people; a mortal danger to people; and
I also think that that's partly why the scientific endeavour—as it's
demolished the traditional underpinnings of our moral systems—has
produced an emergent nihilism and hopelessness among people that
makes them more susceptible to ideological possession. I think it's a
fundamental problem. And I do believe that the highest truths—let's
put it that way—the highest truths are moral truths. I'm thinking
about that from a Darwinian perspective."*

Harris, who is a slippery customer himself, spends most of the interview just trying to nail Peterson down to a coherent definition of
"truth", but has less success than a Republican trying to get Bill Clinton
to define what the meaning of "is" is.

*Harris: I would expect many people will share my frustration that
you're not granting what seem to be, just fairly obvious and undeniable
facts, and now we were having to use this concept of truth in a pretty
inconvenient way, right, because I don't see how anyone is going to
think that it makes sense....*

*Peterson: You know, look, fine, of course it's going to be controversial.
I mean, the claim I'm making is that scientific truth is nested inside*

moral truth. And moral truth is the final adjudicator. And your claim is no, moral truth is nested inside scientific truth, and scientific truth is the final adjudicator. It's like, fine, you know, those are both are coherent positions.

Harris: But yours actually isn't coherent.

Peterson, realizing how badly this exchange made him look, eventually came up with a master plan to explain away his very public philosophical depantsing, which he unveiled on the Joe Rogan show. This turned out to be a spectacularly unwise decision, as he went from the frying pan into the blast furnace with his now-infamously laughable claim to have gone 600 hours without sleep.

What is particularly interesting about Peterson's attempt to cover up his self-immolation at the hands of a media ally is not the inherent absurdity of his claims or the childish nature of his lies, but rather, the way in which he obviously seeks to retroactively revise the narrative of the debate.

His behavior is very much like that of the high school student who receives a disappointing score on the S.A.T. and blames his poor performance on partying too hard the night before, except in Peterson's case, it is more akin to blaming his poor performance on having been abducted and ritually abused for two weeks by demonic time-traveling aliens who returned him to Earth just five minutes before the test.

Lest you think I exaggerate, consider the following dialogue from Peterson's appearance on the Joe Rogan Experience #1139 on July 18, 2018.

Peterson: The worst response I think we're allergic to or allergic whatever the hell this is having an inflammatory response to something called sulfites and we had some apple cider that have sulfites in it and that was really not good like I was done for a month. That was the first time I talked to Sam Harris.

Rogan: You were done for a month?

Peterson: Oh yeah, it took me out for a month it was awful, yeah, yeah.

Rogan: So this is right before this whole truth conversation with Sam Harris that got stuck in the mud.

Peterson: During. During. It was, I think, the day I talked to Sam was like the worst day of my life. Not because of talking to Sam.

Rogan: Just physical.

Peterson: Jesus I was so dead but I didn't want to not do it....

Peterson: There's no way I could have lived like that if that would have lasted for... see Mikayla knew by that point that it would probably only last a month, and I was like-

Rogan: A month! From fucking cider!

Peterson: Well, I didn't sleep that, that month. I didn't sleep for 25 days. I didn't sleep at all. I didn't sleep at all for 25 days.

Rogan: How is that possible?

Peterson: I'll tell you how it's possible. You lay in bed, frozen in something approximating terror for eight hours and then you get up

Ironically, given the likelihood that Rogan was attempting to help Peterson sweep his abysmal performance with Sam Harris under the rug, it was probably his interruption and emphasis on the word "month" that caused Peterson's auto-mirroring habit to kick in and prompt him to apply that particular unit of time to the period of sleeplessness he was intending to declare.

As he did when he was lying about his decision to deplatform Faith Goldy, Peterson demonstrates his customary tell when he describes how he didn't sleep "that, that month" and then repeats his false claim three times.

Again, remember that Jordan Peterson claims to choose his words very, very carefully. But what we are seeing in the Rogan dialogue is the work of a habitual deceiver, a con man in action, constantly scanning his target for clues that he can mirror in order to successfully convince the target of his sincerity and veracity.

The Eighth Principle of Jordanetics:
You can speak a new world into existence through your lies.

Chapter 14

Schroedinger's Rape

Peterson doesn't like the question, "Do you believe in the divinity of Jesus?" for the same reasons he doesn't like the question, "Do you believe in God?" It all depends on what you mean by "believe" and "divinity."

—Dr. Greg Boyd

Rule 9: Assume that the Person You Are Listening To Might Know Something You Don't

A very close reading of Rule 9 is necessary, because due to the deceptive manner in which it is presented, its true nature has been completely missed by Peterson's fans. As usual, the explicit rule appears to consist a very basic truism, namely, the person with whom you are engaged in conversation may possess information that you do not.

This is not merely a safe assumption, it borders on tautology. Literally everyone to whom you speak, and to whom you listen, knows something that you do not, even if it is something as mundane as what the other person ate for breakfast.

Assume that the person you are listening to might know something you don't.

As straightforward as this advice appears to be, nearly every significant word in the sentence proves to have a double meaning.

Peterson begins explaining the Ninth Rule with a long story about a patient who is uncertain as to whether or not she was raped five times. He describes her as being extremely vague and unprepossessing, to the point of being a ghost. At the same time, she was also sufficiently Machiavellian to arrange to be appointed to an important government advisory board despite knowing nothing about government, consulting, or the subject on which she was advising. She had never held a real job, but hosted a radio show about small business, and had been on welfare all her life.

Peterson, understandably, is not terribly sympathetic to this manipulative grifter. It takes one to know one, after all, and by his own account, it soon becomes clear that Peterson has no intention of helping the woman he describes as a denizen of chaos and the underworld, a walking disaster, and Nietzsche's pale criminal. She has no interest in enlightenment and his central Jungian ethic is not to help the tormented in Hell, but merely to study them in order to understand their pain.

Peterson considers his two options: to help her to understand that she was raped, or to help her understand that she was not raped. He considers that the former would simplify her life, but the latter might help her change it. He contemplates his own perspective on the matter, musing that if he was an adherent of a left-wing, social justice ideology, he would tell her that she was raped, but if he were an adherent of a conservative ideology, he would tell her that she was not raped.

And in either case, he declares, her response would prove his judgment to be true, at least, for Petersonian values of truth.

So, as you have probably come to expect by now, Peterson does neither.

He chooses neither the chaos of rape nor the order of not-rape, but instead chooses to merely listen, leaving her in an indeterminate state of Schroedinger's Rape, where she still didn't know if she'd been raped and neither did he.

Life, Jordan Peterson explains, is very complicated. It is especially complicated when one does not know what the meaning of "is" is. But at least, Peterson reassures us, even though he did absolutely nothing and failed to help his patient in any way, she did not leave his office as the living embodiment of what he describes as his damned ideology.

Those are Peterson's own words, his own "damned ideology", and they are revelatory indeed. It's a damning confession too, given how Peterson repeatedly claims to be post-ideological, having left all ideologies behind in response to his despair at the petty envy and superficiality of his fellow socialist Party members.

I had outgrown the shallow Christianity of my youth by the time I could understand the fundamentals of Darwinian theory. After that, I could not distinguish the basic elements of Christian belief from wishful thinking. The socialism that soon afterward became so attractive to me as an alternative proved equally insubstantial.

—12 Rules for Life

But it is not Peterson's ideology that is damnable, it is his philosophy.

Peterson chooses to leave Miss S. in a state of confusion, in a twenty-year hell, never knowing for certain whether she was raped five times or not. But he explains that he does this for her own good. His inaction is justified because the only way that she can obtain the answer that will enlighten her is by crawling through the roots of the underworld and discovering for herself the self-knowledge that is her pragmatic Darwinian, survival-enhancing truth.

What is the utility of the mere objective truth concerning the actual historical fact of what really happened compared to that?

Peterson's Jungian approach to therapy here is unconventional, to put it mildly, and it has considerably more in common with a Scientology auditing session than it does with a conventional counseling session.

Forget the three times Peterson has been accused of sexual improprieties by his students. It's a wonder that he is still allowed to commit psychology on his unsuspecting patients.

So, what does all of this non-therapy have to do with listening to people who might know something you don't? In Peterson's example, Peterson is the listener and Miss S is the person to whom he is listening. It can be assumed that Miss S had to have known the answer to the question that Peterson didn't; she was there on all five occasions and presumably she had at least some inkling of what actually happened each time. Nevertheless, Peterson declares that his patient would have needed to discuss the historical events for at least twenty years in order to figure out whether she had been raped or not.

In fact, he explicitly argues that the truth could not be known, because there is no objective truth of the matter capable of being known.

> *There was no way of knowing the objective truth. And there never would be. There was no objective observer, and there never would be. There was no complete and accurate story. Such a thing did not and could not exist.*

> —*12 Rules for Life*

Notice the subtle contradictions encapsulated here in these five sentences. The truth is that there were, in fact, at least two observers to the objective act of rape or not rape. The fact that they would not necessarily be objective observers is irrelevant to the objective fact of the observed act having taken place or not. Furthermore, the first sentence of the quote clearly implies that an objective truth exists, the problem is merely that it could not be determined due to the lack of objectivity of the observers. Just two sentences later, however, Peterson contradicts himself by asserting that a complete and accurate story, which is to say the objective truth of what happened, did not and could not exist!

The outrageous thing that Peterson is suggesting here is that the thing neither he know his patient knows, the thing that did not and could not exist, is therefore not damaging to his patient. Whatever the long-term damage of these possible rapes might be, it can be ameliorated by a victim's ignorance of the actual facts.

Thus, even if Miss S was raped on one of those five occasions, actually knowing whether she was or was not raped is not particularly important. Whether the acts were real or not, they are now part of her past and she should instead be focused on the future.

But how can she possibly focus on the future when she does not know the foundation for it that the past provides? Furthermore, if the question "Was I raped?" is sufficiently significant for it to consume multiple therapy sessions, let alone 20 years of therapy, how is she supposed to simply ignore it and move on?

On the other hand, Peterson is aware of the possibility that the thing his patient knows that he does not is that she was not actually raped. She is a confirmed grifter, after all, and it is far from impossible that her unknown motive was to entice her psychologist into substantiating a false rape narrative that she had created. Given the fact that Jordan Peterson has thrice been falsely accused of sexual improprieties himself, this would be a possibility that he simply could not rule out.

So Peterson dodges her bullet by listening without even trying to help her clarify what happened to her. While this would be a perfectly reasonable approach if the patient was a liar, Peterson readily admits that he does not know that to be the case. Of course, if she wasn't searching for a false rape accusation, and had, in fact been a five-time rape victim, Peterson's refusal to help her in any substantial way callously condemns the woman to decades of questions, self-condemnation, and emotional insecurity.

How can he possibly justify this inaction and professional irresponsibility? Is it really so important that he is not mistaken for an SJW or a conservative? Is it really so vital that she not be transformed into the embodiment of his damned ideology? What is the point of seeing a psychologist who refuses to help you?

These questions are beyond us. But one that is not is what this very strange episode has to do with the rule about listening, and what, exactly is the nature of the damned ideology from which he is protecting her?

What ideology is so damnable that it would harm someone who has already been raped as many as five times?

The answer is provided by the application of the earlier rules. The patient is the archetype of the low-status lobster. She is a vague, nonexistent denizen of chaos. Whether she has really been victimized or not, she does not merit Peterson's help. Whether he confirms her rape or he establishes her lies, she remains incapable of standing up straight and rising to the more perfect order of the Middle Way.

But now that the reader has advanced further along the 12-Rule Path, Peterson can explain how you can do more than simply extricate yourself from any unseemly connections to low-status friends. Now you can make use of the unfortunate individuals.

First, ensure that the person to whom you are listening is a low-status lobster. He needs to be one who is likely to remain entrapped in the disorder and chaos of Hell below, someone who can't be redeemed or isn't worth redeeming, someone who, in your younger days, before Jordanetics, might have been capable of dragging you down with him.

Second, assume that the individual to whom you are listening is keeping a secret. It's not that the thing he knows may consist of new and useful knowledge, something from which you can learn and grow. To the contrary, the secret he possesses is most likely irrelevant to you. The important thing is that you can use the secret he has shared with you to improve your standing, with him or with others.

Third, do your best to avoid expressing any personal opinion of the secret once it is shared with you. Avoid even mentioning it if you can. By leaving the secret unspoken, and leaving its sharer in the dark about your understanding of his secret, you are now able to exert power over him, and possibly even over others as well, by using your new secret knowledge as leverage. The less you speak about what you know, the more uncertainty you create in the minds of others and the more power you hold over them.

This is why the Ninth Rule necessarily comes so far along the 12-Rule Path, because it consists of a complex application of several of the preceding rules that need to be understood and successfully applied before one can even begin to comprehend it, let alone utilize it. And while it may strike some readers as cruel and exceedingly manipulative, when taken in the context of the preceding rules, it is the natural extension of the narcissistic principles of Jordanetics.

The Ninth Rule would be much better understood if it were worded in a more straightforward manner. Any secret shared with you is a potential means of elevating your standing in the dominance hierarchy. And the way you use knowledge to increase your standing is to keep it to yourself.

Thus, we arrive at another paradox of Jordanetics. Conversation is conspiracy. But the victim of this conspiracy is the person with whom you are having the conversation.

The Ninth Principle of Jordanetics:
Dominate the conversation and control the narrative by keeping
your mouth shut.

Chapter 15

Speaking Madness into Being

I don't know what the Hell I'm talking about.

—Dr. Jordan Peterson

Rule 10: Be Precise in Your Speech

This rule will likely strike the reader of this book as one that borders on parody, given what he now knows about the nature of Peterson's careless and deceit-filled speech. In case it is not entirely obvious from the various quotes from Peterson's books and public appearances scattered throughout the book, Peterson is an almost comically imprecise speaker. Ask ten different Peterson fans what he means by something, and you will almost invariably be provided with at least eight different definitions, most of them contradictory.

There are a whole host of Peterson memes floating around the Internet, but perhaps the most entertaining is a parody of the Nike ad starring ex-NFL quarterback Colin Kaepernick, celebrated for his principled decision to kneel during the national anthem played prior to the kickoff at football games.

The Nike ad says: *Believe in something, even if it means sacrificing everything.*

The Peterson parody says: *It depends on what you mean by believe. It depends on what you mean by sacrifice.*

Throughout the book, Peterson has repeatedly indicated in a variety of ways that he does not believe in anything that can be considered objective reality, but in the chapter devoted to Rule 10, he leaves even the most skeptical reader with no doubts in this regard. For example, because laptop computers eventually become obsolete, Peterson decides that their nature is transient, like the leaf that crumbles and dissolves within a matter of weeks.

Because they can connect to the Internet and run applications hosted elsewhere, laptops can only maintain their "computer-like facade" for but a few short years. I believe that Basho, the great Japanese poet, wrote a haiku concerning this very matter.

Obsolete laptop
Outdated
Are you still even a PC?

What Peterson argues is that because material things decay and become obsolete, they are not really things, or at least not the objects that we superficially consider them to be. He argues, quite literally that a car is neither a thing nor an object, but merely a transportation device.

He briefly considers the grammatical argument to the contrary, but ultimately dismisses it, because what are the mere rules of linguistic grammar to a Master of the Balance who has transcended both objective reality and sanity? Peterson spends several pages redefining objects and things as non-objects and non-things, based on the reasoning that because our perceptions are limited and we do not observe these objects and things with perfect omniscience, they obviously do not exist.

This rule is significant because it explains a central paradox of Jordan Peterson. How can he possibly claim to choose his words very, very carefully when he so often says things that are manifestly absurd? How can he assert the value of truth when telling shameless lies? Why does he urge precision in one's speech when he himself speaks in such a tortuous, meandering, and incoherent manner?

The answer is simple: Peterson is attempting to avoid scaring the women and children with the true nature of his philosophy. The masses are not ready to accept the idea that neither God nor reality nor truth actually exist, therefore it is necessary to very carefully conceal one's true meaning beneath a fog of word-salad that confuses all but the most worthy. In order to maintain his dominance, the philosopher must conceal his secret, because as soon as it is revealed in an straightforward manner, everyone will understand that all Peterson has to offer is warmed-over occult gnosticism. A secret remains at its most powerful when it has not yet been revealed.

But there is even more than this to understand. Now that the nine previous rules have put the postulant of the 12-Rule Path through the philosophical rigors required and prepared him for life, he is ready to face the real challenge of transforming philosophy into a magic that is capable of transforming words into an experiential reality that suits the magician's narrative. Not unlike a wizard counseling his acolyte, Peterson argues that we be very careful of our words as we summon the demons that will impose our will onto existence.

What Peterson is teaching here is the transformation of reality through speech, of changing the world through the magickal combination of word and will.

Crowley expressed the same concept in a more succinct manner: *"MAGICK is the Science and Art of causing Change to occur in conformity with Will."*

James Frazer's classic guide to occult thinking, *The Golden Bough*, explained this particular brand of magic:

> *Whenever sympathetic magic occurs in its pure unadulterated form, it is assumed that in nature one event follows another necessarily and invariably without the intervention of any spiritual or personal agency. Thus its fundamental conception is identical with that of modern science; underlying the whole system is a faith, implicit but real and firm, in the order and uniformity of nature. The magician*

does not doubt that the same causes will always produce the same effects, that the performance of the proper ceremony accompanied by the appropriate spell, will inevitably be attended by the desired results, unless, indeed, his incantations should chance to be thwarted and foiled by the more potent charms of another sorcerer. He supplicates no higher power: he sues the favour of no fickle and wayward being: he abases himself before no awful deity. Yet his power, great as he believes it to be, is by no means arbitrary and unlimited. He can wield it only so long as he strictly conforms to the rules of his art, or to what may be called the laws of nature as conceived by him. To neglect these rules, to break these laws in the smallest particular is to incur failure, and may even expose the unskillful practitioner himself to the utmost peril.

—James Frazer, *The Golden Bough*

Hence the importance of precision. One must be very careful indeed to get all of the words of the spell correct, lest the reality one creates turn out to be even more of a Hell than the one it replaced. Peterson warns of the possibility of error, and advises his metaphorical apprentice how to address a spell gone wrong.

When something goes wrong, even perception itself must be questioned, along with evaluation, thought and action. When error announces itself, undifferentiated chaos is at hand. Its reptilian form paralyzes and confuses. But dragons, which do exist (perhaps more than anything else exists) also hoard gold. In that collapse into the terrible mess of uncomprehended Being lurks the possibility of new and benevolent order. Clarity of thought—courageous clarity of thought—is necessary to call it forth.

It is here that Peterson identifies how the Tenth Rule empowers his student to impose his will upon reality, to give structure to chaos and re-establish order though one's speech. By speaking carefully, by speaking precisely, we can reorder reality to our preference. But should we speak carelessly or imprecisely, the spell will not work. Or worse, it will transform reality into an even more dangerous and hostile place. Crowley's spells were defined in a similar manner.

Illustration: It is my Will to inform the World of certain facts within my knowledge. I therefore take "magical weapons", pen, ink, and paper; I write "incantations"—these sentences—in the "magical language" i.e. that which is understood by the people I wish to instruct; I call forth "spirits", such as printers, publishers, booksellers, and so forth, and constrain them to convey my message to those people. The composition and distribution of this book is thus an act of MAGICK by which I cause Changes to take place in conformity with my Will.

—Aleister Crowley, *MAGICK*

Time and time and time again throughout Rule 10, Peterson asserts that the use of precise and specific words in the face of chaos will prove to be its antidote. Peterson considers precise speech, the sort of speech that makes material manifest, that isolates and separates things from their unknowable histories, to be a white magic. With the Tenth Rule, Peterson provides the initiate with more than just the means to survive amid the suffering of the world, he provides him with the means to transcend the very reality of the world with his words.

**The Tenth Principle of Jordanetics:
Transcend the material world by very carefully choosing the words that will alter its reality.**

Chapter 16

Skateboards and Sacrifice

The mysterious and seemingly irrational "sacrificial" ritual actually dramatizes or acts out two critically important and related ideas: first, that the essence of man—that is, the divine aspect—must constantly be "offered up" to the unknown, must present itself voluntarily to the destructive/creative power that constitutes the Great Mother, incarnation of the unpredictable (as we have seen); and second, that the "thing that is loved best" must be destroyed—that is, sacrificed—in order for the positive aspect of the unknown to manifest itself.

—Dr. Jordan Peterson

Rule 11: Do Not Bother Children When They are Skateboarding

Rule Eleven is a particularly tricky one. Peterson spreads truth liberally in the bait he offers to the casual reader, to the point that even Peterson's most cynical critic may be tempted to give this rule a passing grade. After all, who doesn't agree with the idea of letting kids be kids? But while Peterson has a tendency to play a devious little game of Two Truths and a Lie throughout *12 Rules for Life*, in this chapter he turns that tendency up to literally eleven.

Two Truths and a Lie is a game commonly used to break the ice, in which one person tells everyone three facts about themselves and the rest of the players try to guess which one is not true. It is a good way to learn some memorable things about a person, but the game would not be much of a game if the player never revealed their lie to the others. Instead of breaking the ice and learning a couple of interesting facts about a person, everyone would be left with nothing but possibly false narratives about one another.

His opening story concerns a group of reckless skateboarders near his workplace, and how the University of Toronto was able to put a stop to them in the name of safety, by installing skatestoppers, whose "sheer harsh ugliness … makes a lie of the reasons for its implementation."

Identifying this bureaucratic urge to control skateboarders as a sort of Jungian evil twin of public safety and public concern, he illustrates how the "social justice-dispensing front" is more concerned with looking good than in doing good. He writes how *The Road to Wigan Pier*, by George Orwell, was a socialist critique of the average educated socialist, who was usually much less concerned for the poor than he was jealous of the rich.

This behavior can be described as the evil twin in action. A passionate, even selfless cause often serves as cover for a different, more nefarious motive. Peterson reminds the reader of Jung's admonition, which he describes as a surgically wicked psychoanalytic dictum, which is to look at the consequences and infer the motivation if you are puzzled as to why someone did something.

Peterson's point is, on its face, a fairly obvious one. Just because someone says they are acting from high principles for the good of others, there is no reason to take them at face value. That's true, just as there is no reason to believe someone who says he is choosing his words very, very carefully or considering the matter for the first time is necessarily telling the truth.

So what is the secret purpose of Rule 11, if it is not simply about leaving boys free to skateboard where they want? It is about facing your own evil twin. And who is your evil twin? Why, it is none other than your former self. It is you, before you rose above the Chaos. It is you, when you were still trapped by your limiting friendships. It is you, before you learned to cast spells. In short, it is you before you learned how to apply Peterson's *12 Rules for Life*.

Peterson confirms this reading in his subsequent illustrative examples. He follows the example of the anti-skater bureaucrat with his broken, homicidal, suicidal friend Chris, an anti-human professor's lecture, and finishes with the world-hating Columbine shooters. These archetypical evil twins are people who claimed they wanted to make the world a better place, but went about it by taking negative action against the world's inhabitants.

Chris, Peterson's childhood friend, is the most obvious expression of Peterson's own evil twin and former self. Chris comes from the same background as Peterson, experienced the sympathetic antagonism with the local Natives, struggled to escape their small town, pursued the same woman, and battled the same dangerous and deadly mental illness as Peterson. Chris's life directly mirrored Peterson's life, and it was not until Peterson metaphorically left him behind for good following Chris's suicide that he finally managed to dispell his evil twin's presence.

The evil twin is not only the negative mirror of the enlightened being, he is a symbol of that being's death. Peterson calls them self-appointed judges of the human race; they are the speakers behind the critical voices with whom you must negotiate as per the Fourth Rule: compare yourself to who you were yesterday, not to who someone else is today

The goal is to put the evil twin behind you, once and for all. But what does that mean? To understand that, we must first grasp the origin of the self as mirrored twins, the children of the ancient symbol of the Terrible Mother that Peterson spends so much of this chapter discussing.

The Terrible Mother is Tiamat. She is the mother of all things, she gives birth to both men and gods. She is Nature, she is the Unknown, and she is Chaos. She is the spirit of carelessness and of unconsciousness; she is represented by the dragon and by the snake, both of whom dwell in the Underworld. So, obviously, she represents oppression, specifically oppression of a female variety.

His point here is that society will create monsters out of healthy men if it tries too hard to control them. This is not a particularly deep insight, considering that Princess Leia made a similar observation to the Grand Moff Tarkin in the movie *Star Wars*, but it is extremely informative to see how Peterson describes these monsters, as harsh, fascist, supporters of Donald Trump and the sinister far-right parties on the rise in Holland, Sweden, and Norway.

Even worse, we are informed they particularly enjoy the movies *Iron Man* and *Fight Club*, which tells the reader who is familiar with the actual novel by Chuck Palahniuk that the famous psychiatrist genuinely doesn't know the latter is not about fighting or fascism, but a metaphorical journey into the homosexual underground.

So, your evil twin is a tyrant, a God-Emperor, a fascist with a friendly face. It is not openly evil, it does not display itself as an ideological, murderous, right-wing nationalist wearing lightning bolts and swastikas. Instead, this excessively masculine evil dresses itself up as a bleeding heart, radical Leftist.

Your evil twin is inclined to commit evil in the name, but not the spirit, of proper Leftist motives. Your true self is more naturally liberal, sensitive but not radical, moderate, not extreme. Right wing nationalism is naked evil, usually in reaction to the absence of healthy leftism and the oppressive presence of unhealthy leftism.

Frazer's *The Golden Bough* emphasizes the importance of sacrifice and the human scapegoat in antiquity. The scapegoat, according to Frazer, took many forms, and its rituals varied from culture to culture and situation to situation. It was not always a human being, it was not always a living thing. In fact, the scapegoat was not necessarily even a material thing! But the general concept was that the scapegoat was always used as a means of using a substitute to purge evil from the individual or the community. In other words, a scapegoat was either a lure to draw demons or other evil spirits out of a person or place, or an innocent creature, person or thing that served as a symbol for evil, but at its highest form, it always represented a holy human sacrifice. In other words, even if the scapegoat was a literal goat, its slaughter, symbolic or actual, represented the death of a priest-king or even a god.

When *The Golden Bough* was originally published, it caused great scandal, primarily because in the midst of all the pagan rites and folk tales, it included an entire chapter on Jesus Christ and the Crucifixion. Scholars and theologians alike excoriated the text for its shoddy historicity and the faithful correctly recognized it as blasphemy. Later editions removed the chapter on Christianity, but the original implication that Jesus Christ was merely another archetype of the Dying God motif remains.

Many anthropologists of his time attacked Frazer for his poor scholarship, but he defended his work as mere speculation and hoped it would eventually be replaced by more soundly grounded successor. But it was not. *The Golden Bough*'s influence, both as a work of the occult and of creative expression, remains to this day, and Frazier's interpretation of the scapegoat, including the idea that Jesus Christ was nothing more than the echo of an ancient pagan ritual, are among its most persistent falsehoods.

The significance here is that human sacrifice, or, more specifically, a particular kind of human sacrifice serving as a quasi-divine scapegoat, is the pinnacle of the esoteric magick used in occult spellcasting influenced by Frazier's work.

Being an esotericist himself, Jordan Peterson meditates on sacrifice throughout the *12 Rules for Life*, and his primary example is human sacrifice. Peterson emphasizes that this sort of human sacrifice is the opposite of what he regards as proper sacrifice, but acknowledges that even a proper sacrifice, if a failure, could result in cold-blooded, religion-motivated, bloody murder.

In Jordanetics, human sacrifice of the holy innocent is both the lowest evil and the highest good. As Above, So Below. Recall what

Peterson says of the near-homicides that occurred in his house, due to the supernaturally unsettling presence of Chris, his mirrored self and evil twin.

The spirit of Cain had visited our house, but we were left unscathed.

—12 Rules for Life

Peterson has already established himself as a Christ-figure through his sufferings in the desert and his visions of crucifixion. He has established Chris as his evil twin.

And in his final, self-destructive act, Chris-Cain serves as the archetypical scapegoat, the human sacrifice that purges the evil from the Jordan-Christ.

The symbolic ritual of human sacrifice has other important roles to play in Jordanetics. It includes this kind of duality: where the sacrifice may be proper or improper, committed by unholy Chris or performed on holy Chris. But it is more than that. The "dying god" sacrificed, slaughtered, dead, and reborn, of course, doesn't have to be a sentient entity. It could be a mammoth (which is a "god" because it is viewed as a gift from God or a god), it could be harvested grain (which symbolizes the vision-giving fruit-gift from the serpent and/or God). It could be one's personal ambition in exchange for a social good. Peterson's examples are numerous, but his chief illustration of the occult "dying god" scapegoat is in what he calls Jesus Christ/Horus, the Word. Jesus Christ is portrayed as the "good" sacrifice, of the proper type. Just as Abel is is the "good, ideal and innocent" sacrifice, but Cain's part in it is the "evil, vengeful and improper." That means that such a good sacrifice of the Word has a mirror, an evil twin. Peterson views the Holocaust as that other side.

The Holocaust is deemed an evil and improper sacrifice, just as Cain's slaying of Abel to spite God was evil and improper. But more ominously, more troubling, Peterson declares that the great human sacrifice of the Holocaust fulfilled a holy purpose. There was a spiritual reason for it:

> *It is something more like atonement for the criminal fact of your fractured and damaged Being. It's payment of the debt you owe for the insane and horrible miracle of your existence. It's how you remember the Holocaust. It's how you make amends for the pathology of history. It's adoption for the responsibility for being a potential denizen of Hell. It is willingness to serve as an angel of Paradise.*
>
> —*12 Rules for Life*

From Peterson's dualistic perspective, it ultimately doesn't matter whether the Holocaust was a good and proper sacrifice or an evil and improper one. What matters is that the sacrifice is *remembered*, that the burnt offering of millions of innocents, regardless of the evil motive behind it, redeems the Being of the Spirit of Man, and reconnects those who remember it to the soaring, detached freedom of the skies above the pyramids.

The cornerstone of Peterson's philosophy is that suffering is real, and that taking action that causes suffering is wrong. So, whether Peterson's self-confessed obsession with the Holocaust is ultimately satanic or saintly, the important thing is that the sacrifice occurred, so that it could be remembered. When Peterson recognizes his own capacity to torture children in a dungeon, he is projecting himself into the place of the pagan high priest during the ritual human sacrifice of the dying god.

So, to summarize, your evil twin is your former self, the identity from which you have dissociated yourself. You are the good twin, the enlightened being, the positive side of the mirror. If you have followed the rules very carefully, refrained from action, and chosen your words with sufficient precision, then you have thwarted the God Emperor within, and now it falls to you to defend and uphold a society that thwarts the Chaos of tyrants and identity politics and nationalism. This can only be done by sacrificing the evil twin.

You can't actually kill your evil twin of course. It's bad luck to break mirrors and your evil twin is protected by its ability to hide in your past. Even so, you can't just let it rattle the bars of its psychological prison until eventually it breaks free and unmakes all of your hard-earned progress along the Middle Way. The imperative of the Eleventh Rule is a ritual sacrifice, not a literal one, and the sacrifice involved refers to the integration of the former self with its successor, resulting in a Being that is finally in Balance.

To explain this integration, Peterson refers to the old Charles Atlas ads in the back of comic books, where the weakling hero Mac is publicly bullied and rendered undesirable to women, but after working out, he defeats his former bullies and wins the affections of the girl. Mac's evil twin is not the bully, but rather his former self, the weakling. And so we see that integration is transformation.

As with so many other concepts, Peterson derived this rule of transformation through integration from Jung, who considered this question of integrating good and evil at length in his alchemical studies.

For, as long as Satan is not integrated, the world is not healed and man is not saved. But Satan represents evil, and how can evil be integrated? There is only one possibility: to assimilate it, that is to say, raise it to the level of consciousness. This is done by means of a very complicated symbolic process which is more or less identical with the psychological process of individuation. In alchemy this is called the conjunction of two principles.

—Carl Jung, *Memories, Dreams, Reflections*

So, what Peterson actually means by "don't bother children" is "don't sacrifice children to the gods", which really means fixing the world through assimilation rather than action.

The Eleventh Principle of Jordanetics:
Heal the world by assimilating its evil.

Chapter 17

How a Saint Surmounts Suffering

Evil requires sacrifices. Evil gets off on an individual's willingness to give up life. It's a craving of your own sacrifice. You have to make the choice or else evil doesn't appreciate it. The free will requirement of good is very similar to evil. If you don't give up your own integrity or your own righteousness, or the love of your family, evil isn't really as interested in it. They're trying to get you to choose it.

—Owen Benjamin

Rule 12: Pet a cat when you encounter one on the street

The final rule in *12 Rules for Life* in many ways exemplifies Peterson's Jungian practice of suspending his critical judgment. While he has toyed with the poor, overmatched reader all throughout the book, here he is at his most brazen, changing his definitions and subjects around with the casual ease of a Las Vegas blackjack dealer distributing cards, whipsawing his bewildered audience, most of whom by now have been battered into numbed intellectual submission.

If you harbor a cruel streak and want to amuse yourself, ask a Peterson fan to explain the Twelfth Rule to you. The look of confusion and dismay when it dawns upon them that they retain literally nothing from the climactic chapter of this book they hold to be so meaningful is what the beginning of knowledge looks like.

Again, as the cynic has come to anticipate, even though cats are the object of Rule 12, Peterson spends most of the chapter focusing on dogs instead. He does this, he explains, because he doesn't wish to be found guilty of minimal group identification, a phenomenon we are informed was discovered by a social psychologist named Henri Tajfel.

It's important to observe that while Peterson refuses to recognize the objective reality of mundane non-things such as "laptop computers" and the transportation devices known as "cars", historical events such as "rape" or "the Crucifixion", let alone more abstract concepts such as "truth", "Jesus", and "God", he believes very strongly in the reality of ideas that spring out of the imagination of 19th and 20th century European psychologists.

Tafjel is chiefly known for analyzing the intellectual aspects of prejudice and social identity theory, which is another way of saying that he was a Polish Jew obsessed with producing a scientific-sounding explanation for why the World War II-era Germans hated the Jews. Wikipedia informs us that Tafjel believed social psychologists should seek to address serious social problems by examining how psychological dimensions interact with historical, ideological, and cultural factors, which goes a long way towards explaining why Peterson regards him as an authority.

Peterson elaborates on the psychological studies that claim to demonstrate two things that are seemingly contradictory. On the one hand, people are social, on the other, people are antisocial. People are social because they like the members of their own group. People are antisocial because they don't like the members of other groups. Recall, however, that Peterson wants you to be wary of groups, that it is only the individual who ultimately matters. So, Peterson's dualist perspective comes in handy here. As you have probably already ascertained, being social represents Order, while being antisocial represents Chaos. This is our confirmation that Peterson is engaging in the usual esoteric double-talk in which the superficial meaning applies to the normal reader, but holds a deeper meaning for the enlightened initiate.

Peterson is barely even trying to hide his double-talk at this point, as he asserts that the discovery of minimal conditions in the 1950s explains why he began a cat-related chapter with a description of his dog, and promptly began talking about a third and unrelated subject. Even the most generous reader who still doubts the existence of the mystical level of Peterson's book will be forced to admit here that Peterson has become utterly incoherent as he descends into bafflegarble.

This is the one point at which even Peterson's most loyal fans will tend to agree with him when he declares that he doesn't know what the Hell he is talking about.

And it's not even correct for Peterson to describe the chapter as being cat-related, as he devotes all of three paragraphs to the behavior of cats and the benefits of petting them. If you still don't understand that Peterson is not writing about what he pretends to be writing about, I don't know what more could possibly be cited to convince you than this example of Peterson simply not writing about cats at all.

In any case, it is because of Tajfel's minimal-conditions discovery that I began this cat-related chapter with a description of my dog. Otherwise, the mere mention of a cat in the title would be enough to turn many dog people against me, just because I didn't include canines in the group of entities that should be petted. Since I also like dogs, there is no reason for me to suffer such a fate. So, if you like to pet dogs when you meet them on the street, don't feel obliged to hate me. Rest assured, instead, that this is also an activity of which I approve. I would also like to apologize to all the cat people who now feel slighted, because they were hoping for a cat story but had to read all this dog-related material. Perhaps they might be satisfied by some assurance that cats do illustrate the point I want to make better, and that I will eventually discuss them. First, however, to other things.

—*12 Rules for Life*

His concerns that he might annoy the cat-loving reader, while overly dramatic, are not entirely misplaced. Although the lack of connection between the promise implied in the rule and what is delivered in the text of the chapter is standard practice throughout each of the 12 Rules, there is simply no connection at all between the subject of this Rule for Life and the chapter itself. Lobsters may not share common ancestry with humans and the asserted implications of their dominance hierarchy for the human social hierarchy may not be as relevant as Peterson believes, but at least Peterson spends some time actually discussing lobsters in the lobster-related chapter. He may not give a single example of picking friends who want the best for him in, but at least he shows the depressing consequences of his having chosen poorly in the friend-related chapter. He may criticize the world despite his own house being in imperfect order, in violation of his own Sixth Rule, but at least he discusses houses in the house-related chapter.

But even the most generous reader cannot let Peterson off the hook in this cat-related chapter, because whatever their merits may be, and whatever benefits petting them might bring, cats are not dogs, and they definitely are not his daughter Mikhaila.

Peterson's autobiographical perspective intensifies here, as he shares with his reader the agonizing pain his beloved daughter suffered throughout her childhood as a result of severe polyarticular juvenile idiopathic arthritis affecting no less than 37 of her joints. She spent most of her childhood heavily medicated, beginning with codeine, then moved up to oxycontin when the codeine proved insufficient to control her pain. She was injected with drugs usually used in chemotherapy, Enbrel and Methotrexate, to suppress her immune system, and was prescribed an SSRI antidepressant called Cipralex for severe depression and anxiety at age 12.

She actually ended up in a wheelchair at one point, before finally being forced to get her hip and ankle replaced at the age of 17.

His daughter's health catastrophe devastates the entire Peterson family. They are forced to traverse an underworld of almost unmitigated pain and suffering, a Hell where every unexpected turn proves to be a bad one. Understandably, it causes Peterson to further question the faith he'd rejected as a child, as he wonders what sort of sadistic God would create such a hellish world where such a things could happen, especially to an innocent and happy little girl.

And then, for seemingly no reason whatsoever, Peterson abruptly switches away from his daughter's litany of health disasters to a discussion of the 1938 creation of the cultural icon of Superman. But rather than, as might be expected, addressing the tragic roots of the comic book hero, who is believed to have been born of a son's grief for his father, killed in a 1932 armed robbery, Peterson focuses on the terminal *deus ex machina* which tended to render an overpowered Superman boring to fans of the character.

It is not until Superman is stripped of his more significant powers, such as his ability to shake off a nuclear attack or move an entire planet, does his story become interesting again. Being, Peterson concludes, appears to require limits.

And furthermore, those limits apply to human reason as well.

Something supersedes thinking, despite its truly awesome power. When existence reveals itself as existentially intolerable, thinking collapses in on itself. In such situations—in the depths—it's noticing, not thinking, that does the trick. Perhaps you might start by noticing this: when you love someone, it's not despite their limitations. It's because of their limitations. Of course, it's complicated. You don't have to be in love with every shortcoming, and merely accept. You shouldn't stop trying to make life better, or let suffering just be. But there appear to be limits on the path to improvement beyond which we might not want to go, lest we sacrifice our humanity itself.

—12 Rules for Life

The good news is that Mikhaela not only survives her long battle with mental and physical illness, she goes on to marry, have a child, and even to launch a career as a dietary con woman overselling the merits of an Atkins-style meat-only diet to cure a long litany of mental and physical ills, including, but not limited to: inflammation, gum disease, rheumatoid arthritis, autoimmune disease, excess weight, brain fog, anxiety, diabetes, ankylosing spondylitis, other types of arthritis, high blood pressure, depression and fatigue.

Considering what the young woman has been through, even a hardened skeptic like myself cannot find the necessary wherewithal to criticize or condemn her. And given the current percentage of the American and Canadian publics that are dangerously obese, it can be convincingly argued that whatever the shortcomings of the Mikhaela Diet might be, the benefits it has to offer a dangerously overweight society stuffing itself on far too many carbohydrates and sugars significantly outweigh them.

Peterson closes the chapter by finally getting around to discussing the titular cats. The significance of cats to him is that they are a pure form of Being, and more importantly, they are a manifestation of nature that actually approves of humanity. He suggests, therefore, that petting a cat is a reminder of the wonders of Being that make up for the ineradicable suffering that accompanies it.

The Twelfth Principle of Jordanetics:
To lift the world out of Hell, you must be willing to accept its pain and suffering into yourself.

Chapter 18

The Magickal Pen of Light

I'm a bad guy but I'm trying not to be and that's fucking something....

—Dr. Jordan Peterson

Peterson has a lot of dreams and visions. He presents them as messages. Sometimes they are messages of hope. Sometimes they are dreadful warnings. But whenever he describes one, he never bothers to explain what he believes its meaning to be. He may go off onto a tangent he believes relates to the vision, but not even once does he follow up a vision with an interpretation. Every time he brings up a vision, he does so in a manner that indicates he intends for it to illustrate something to the reader, but it always winds up coming off as a secret that he intends to keep to himself.

That's because it is.

One of the principles Peterson repeatedly asserts is to look at the consequences and determine a motive from them. This idea originally comes from Jung, but Peterson exercises it naturally and frequently throughout the *12 Rules for Life*. With that metric in mind, consider the motive behind Peterson's account of seeing a friend make use of a pen that emitted light from the tip so that one could write with it in the dark.

Peterson, of course, views this device as deeply symbolic and meaningful in a personal sense, since he sees himself as a bringer of light to a humanity that is lost in darkness, so Peterson asks the friend to give him the pen. e is, by his own account, inordinately pleased when his friend dutifully obliges.

His new ability to write illuminated words in the darkness delights Peterson. Taken with the psychographic power of what he describes as his Newfound Pen of Light, Peterson begins to ask questions of the pen and scribble down the answers it provides. When he describes being surprised by some of the mystical answers that he writes, it is clear that the insights he is recording are not his own. This is what is known as automatic writing. The approach is similar to the operator of a Ouija board, in which the inquirer asks the questions consciously, but the answers purport to be provided without his conscious thought.

Automatic writing or psychography is an alleged psychic ability allowing a person to produce written words without consciously writing. The words are claimed to arise from a subconscious, spiritual or supernatural source.

Automatic writing as a spiritual practice was reported by Hyppolyte Taine in the preface to the third edition of his "De l'intelligence", published in 1878. Besides "etherial visions" or "magnetic auras", Fernando Pessoa claimed to have experienced automatic writing. He said he felt "owned by something else", sometimes feeling a sensation in the right arm which he claimed was lifted into the air without his will. William Fletcher Barrett wrote that "Automatic messages may take place either by the writer passively holding a pencil on a sheet of paper, or by the planchette, or by a 'ouija board'. In spiritualism, spirits are claimed to take control of the hand of a medium to write messages, letters, and even entire books. Automatic writing can happen in a trance or waking state.

—*Wikipedia*

A famous early episode of automatic writing came during the creation of Enochian magic, in the 16th century. Occultists John Dee and Sir Edward Kelly used automatic writing to discover the celestial language of angels, which they referred to as the first language of God-Christ.

Another practitioner of automatic writing was the poet and author William Butler Yeats. He called it the Automatic Script. He utilized it extensively throughout his life. At first, he believed he was communing with the dead, but as he advanced in the practice, Yeats came to believe that the spirits he was drawing upon were, in fact, forms of his higher self. The most famous product of his deep automatic writing was *Second Coming*, which features the esoteric symbol of the gyre. The gyre is a three-dimensional spiral, which, in motion, forms a pyramid. It represents the movement from the earthly below of the everyday world to the pinnacle of enlightenment above.

Through his automatic writing, Yeats discovered that the highest form of combined gyre represented the spirit. This gyre set named by Yeats as the Diamond and the Hourglass because that is what they looked like, combined. This combination of gyres has eight directional points, similar to the cross of Scientology.

Peterson is clearly familiar with both Yeats and *Second Coming*, as he cites it in Rule 10: Be precise in your speech.

What you least want to encounter will make itself manifest when you are weakest and it is strongest. And you will be defeated.

Turning and turning in the widening gyre
The falcon cannot hear the falconer;
Things fall apart; the centre cannot hold;
Mere anarchy is loosed upon the world,
The blood-dimmed tide is loosed, and everywhere
The ceremony of innocence is drowned;
The best lack all conviction, while the worst
Are full of passionate intensity.

—William Butler Yeats, "The Second Coming"

Also similar to the cross of Scientology is the *Crux Ansata*, better known as the Rosy Cross of the Rosicrucian Order. According to Thelema, Aleister Crowley's psycho-spiritual religion, the cross's two parts are merged together, forming eight directional points. And the symbol of the 8-pointed Golden Dawn cross shares so much in common with the cross of Scientology, that it is difficult for the average person to tell them apart. There is no great mystery as to why; L. Ron Hubbard, the founder of Scientology, praised Aleister Crowley as a great influence on him, and prior to founding Scientology was a member of Crowley's Ordo Templi Orientalis.

The rose at the center of the Rosy Cross symbolizes the ever-expanding goddess of the night named Nuit. The cross itself is called Hadit, the Lord of the Sky, who is the atomically contracted point of all things. These female and male components provide the believer the means with which to demonstrate the godhead of his nature through the contemplation of opposites.

And we're back to the Middle Way and the Balance. Again.

Pyramids, gyres, rosy crosses. Psychology, spiritualism, mysticism, occultic poetry and pagan magicks. How are they all related? Peterson again quotes Yeats in the poem that at first glance appears to be about the Second Coming of Jesus Christ, but actually anticipates the Antichrist. The images of the rocking cradle and the rough beast slouching ominously towards Bethlehem better anticipate the films *Rosemary's Baby* and *The Omen* than Jesus Christ's martial return accompanied by all the Hosts of Heaven.

Peterson does not quote from Yeats simply because he enjoys the man's poetry. In addition to being a talented wordsmith, William Butler Yeats was the great occult rival of Aleister Crowley. In 1900, Yeats, like Crowley, was a member of the Hermetic Order of the Golden Dawn. Yeats, who himself had been kicked out of the occult Theosophical Society for experimenting too much with magic, was among the people in Golden Dawn who found Crowley's magick too dark for their tastes, so they kicked him out of the group. Crowley took great

exception to this and targeted Yeats with several black magick attacks
that eventually culminated in Yeats conjuring a vampire and sending it
after Crowley.

Or so it is reported. Now, however ridiculous you may find this
stuff, the late gentlemen certainly believed it, and Jordan Peterson at
least appears to believe it too. He observably knows a lot more about it
than he does about biology or Christian theology, anyhow.

Both Yeats and Crowley believed that the Taoist concept of Yin and
Yang was a complementary symbol of the Rosy Cross, and Yeats explic-
itly tied his idea of gyres to the same concept. As you already know,
Peterson's 12 rules are heavily focused on finding and maintaining the
Taoist Balance, and cover of his first book, *Maps of Meaning*, features
abstract artwork that portrays the eight points of the *Crux Ansata*.

Peterson's Newfound Pen of Light, which as per his habitual dishonesty was not, in fact, found, but given in response to his blandishments,
must be reconsidered in light of these long-established esoteric practices.
The first question he asks the pen is what he is to do with it.

After a lengthy discourse into the Bible, the nature of prayer, and
Peterson's ideas why God does not answer all prayers literally, he tells
us that the pen's first response is to tell him to write down the words he
wants inscribed on his soul.

However, Peterson completely ignores this response, as instead of
writing down something meaningful, such as "Roll Tide," "John 3:16",
or even "Hail Abraxas, Prince of Hell, Devourer of Worlds, Great Beast
Incarnate and Dark Liege of the Unholy Army of the Dead," he simply
treats his magick pen as if it were a gypsy fortune teller.

What shall I do tomorrow? What shall I do next year? What shall I
do with my life? What shall I do with my wife? What shall I do with
the stranger? What shall I do with the torn nation?

Peterson is again signaling his Messiah complex and his dream to
become the Healer of the Nations. He doesn't recognize that the nations
are tearing themselves apart because of the very globalist ideology to
which he owes his allegiance. And not even a magick pen can tell him

how to repair the torn nation and stitch it back together by utilizing the very ideas that divided it in the first place.

It is only at the very end of the book, in this Coda to his 12-Rule Path for life, that Peterson finally feels able to openly express his true purpose and announce his place among the pantheon of secret bodhisattvas on the Middle Way to Balance and Enlightenment.

It should be clear by now that the 12 principles of Jordanetics are not just a spiritual gift that Peterson bestows upon his readers, they are also the rules for societal survival that the madman has applied to his own life. For the astute reader, the primary takeaway from *12 Rules for Life* should be a profound sense of dismay. Because it is readily apparent that despite all of the very lengthy contemplations and very, very careful articulations, Jordan Peterson's rules have not worked very well for Peterson himself.

His autobiographical episodes are almost universally negative, ranging from the mildly depressing to the outright tragic. He has no friends, he has no peers, he has not surrounded himself with people who want the best for him. He spends far more time, space, and energy on telling us about his failures than about any of his successes. The book is chaotic and incoherent, full of vague and imprecise digressions, where the details don't match up and the stories don't check out. One is left with the impression that Peterson's rules are useless for anyone who is remotely healthy and are very likely to cause more harm than good for the normal, but low-status young men who could really use some good advice for how to live their lives.

And worse, for those readers who are mentally unwell, the *12 Rules for Life* will tend to feed the delusions of those who are already caught up in their imaginary subjective realities where they are not social rejects, but Secret Kings who see themselves as the real victors in every conflict or encounter.

So the inevitable question is: why? Why does Peterson write his rules for life in this dualistic manner, prosaic and useless on one level and esoteric and eccentric on the other. If he feels the need to promote an occultic spiritualism in the mode of Jung, Crowley, Yeats, and Hubbard, why not just come out and do so? It is not as if the Spanish Inquisition is going to burn him at the stake like Galileo or Giordano Bruno. There are four obvious reasons:

1. Many intelligent readers are naturally very skeptical of esoteric teachings. The prophet treating his Newfound Pen of Light like a ouija board has no doubt paid a price in the past for speaking plainly about his whacky notions and quasi-religious nonsense. So, as a true believer in esoteric spiritualism, perhaps he has learned that the best approach with intelligent, independent-minded followers is one that buries its truths in misleading metaphors and confusing narratives.

2. Esoteric teachings, by nature, are convoluted, secretive, and masked by double-meanings. The very term Gnosticism refers directly to secret knowledge. Carl Jung's *Red Book*, from which Peterson draws some of his own principles, was never published in his lifetime. In fact, it was such a private journal of collected esoterica that only very few of his closest associates ever saw any of its contents. It was never intended for general publication, and his legacy-keepers prevented it from being published for decades after his death.

3. The 12-Rule Path, being by nature esoteric, serves as a ritual of recognition for the highly enlightened. Many will come to the secret knowledge, but only the elite individuals capable of transcending the chaos of the lower masses and the ordered pyramids of the dominant in order to achieve their all-seeing status will understand it.

4. The 12-Rule Path serves a dual purpose:

   (a) the occult training of Peterson's most elite followers on their individual paths to spiritual enlightenment;

(b) the establishment of Peterson as the secret prophet of the cult of Jordanetics. He has used these rules to cope with his personal madness, and having done so, has established himself as a messianic shepherd capable of gathering others struggling with clinical depression and delusions around him.

Peterson, the self-anointed visionary, descends into the Chaos of the oppressed, like the Crucified Christ harrowing Hell. Holding the rules for the 12-Rule Path of the Middle Way, he metaphorically offers himself as both a sacrifice and a savior to those willing to follow him out of Chaos and help him restore the Balance.

And if they do as he has done, and seek as he has sought, he promises them a world that will bend, slowly and over time, to their will.

Chapter 19

The Cult of Jordanetics

Is it any wonder that there should be failing and error, not in the highest, the intellectual, Principle, but in Souls that are like undeveloped children?

—Plotinus, *Against the Gnostics*

Jordan Peterson is mentally ill and many of his followers suffer from depression, anxiety, and other forms of mental illness. This is why it is hard for mentally healthy individuals to understand the strength of his appeal. It can be very hard for normal, well-adjusted people to begin to understand how those who are mentally unstable, imbalanced, or otherwise unwell to fall for such obvious lunacy.

Falling into a cult can observably be surprisingly easy. I don't pretend to understand anything about the underlying psychology of those who do, but the mechanism for capturing cultists is fairly straightforward. First, the cult has to provide the potential cultist with assistance. Then it gradually builds trust, in both the leader and the cult itself. Then it convinces the potential cultist, now a novice, to commit to something false. It repeats this process in cycles, initiating the newcomer into falsehood after falsehood, until the initiate is spending most of his life living a lie, to such a degree that admitting to any of the lies means rejecting most of what has become his life.

The NXIVM cult started by Keith Raniere, now being investigated for its illegal money laundering and sex slavery, is replete with astonishing stories of women voluntarily submitting to branding and sexual servitude for the sake of the organization. Raniere was so successful in convincing his followers of his delusional reality that wealthy heiresses and Hollywood actresses not only raised tens of millions of dollars for it, but even corrupted the Personal Emissary for Peace for the Dalai Lama.

To expand its membership, the NXIVM cult provided both free and paid courses for self-improvement to attract initiates. This is similar to Scientology. The free courses are offered in the early stages and the paid courses gradually rise in cost over time as the believer gets deeper and deeper into it.

Jordanetics presently appears to be in the early stages of this approach, as Peterson is already charging hundreds of dollars for VIP Meet & Greet upgrades to his tours, which include "Meet & Greet Event with Jordan Peterson, One Photo with Jordan Peterson, and One Exclusive VIP Laminate."

While Peterson may be content with his multiple revenue streams of book sales, online self-help services, personality assessments, lectures, and speaking tours, the past history of self-help crazes tends to indicate that he will not. He is, after all, on a mission to save the world. It is more likely that, like Dianetics transforming into Scientology, Jordanetics will eventually transform into a pseudo-religious New Age globalist cult.

Isn't this a little paranoid? Not at all. Jordanetics already has two of the three elements required for destructive cult formation in place. According to psychiatrist Robert Jay Lifton, cults can be identified by three characteristics:

> 1. *A charismatic leader who increasingly becomes an object of worship as the general principles that may have originally sustained the group lose their power;*

2. A process I call coercive persuasion or thought reform;

3. The economic, sexual, and other exploitation of group members by the leader and the ruling coterie. "

—*The Harvard Mental Health Letter Volume 7, Number 8* February 1981, reprinted in *AFF News Vol. 2 No. 5*, 1996

There is a fourth element that inevitably tends to be in place when these cults are formed. What does the leader of the cult say of Jesus Christ. Does he say anything about Jesus at all? How does he describe Jesus? As it happens, Jung, Crowley, Hubbard and Peterson all describe Jesus Christ in very similar fashion, to such an extent that when comparing their perspectives, it is very hard to distinguish Peterson's from the other esotericists who regard Christ as a powerful mystic symbol.

The central ideas of Christianity are rooted in Gnostic philosophy, which, in accordance with psychological laws, simply had to grow up at a time when the classical religions had become obsolete. It was founded on the perception of symbols thrown up by the unconscious individuation process which always sets in when the collective dominants of human life fall into decay. At such a time there is bound to be a considerable number of individuals who are possessed by archetypes of a numinous nature that force their way to the surface in order to form new dominants.

This state of possession shows itself almost without exception in the fact that the possessed identify themselves with the archetypal contents of their unconscious, and, because they do not realize that the role which is being thrust upon them is the effect of new contents still to be understood, they exemplify these concretely in their own lives, thus becoming prophets and reformers.

In so far as the archetypal content of the Christian drama was able to give satisfying expression to the uneasy and clamorous unconscious of the many, the consensus omnium raised this drama to a universally binding truth—not of course by an act of judgment, but by the irrational fact of possession, which is far more effective.

Thus Jesus became the tutelary image or amulet against the archetypal powers that threatened to possess everyone.

—Maps of Meaning: The Architecture of Belief

Peterson's visions of himself as crucified messiah atop the pyramids of the All-Seeing Eye of Horus may only be harmless metaphors or an unconscious Freudian expression of his sexual desire for his relatives, but as anyone who has criticized Peterson knows very well, he is a weirdly charismatic man whose followers only support him more fervently when his mistakes are exposed. The 12-Rule Path is a guide for reshaping one's thought processes and its deceptive, dualistic techniques are designed to manipulate the reader into something deeper than mere self-help.

Futhermore, Peterson has already created a system of fee-based self-authoring services capable of serving as an isolating infrastructure of systematic exploitation in the style of Scientology and NXVIM courses. And as a psychologist, he knows very well that Man, even godless post-Christian Man, needs religion. Even if he does not call it religion, Man needs something upon which to build his belief systems.

If religion is erased, something must be put in its place. Belief systems are intrinsic to human intelligence and survival. They "frame" the flux of primary experience, which would otherwise flood the mind.

—Camille Paglia

Constructing the basis for a new world religion would certainly explain why Jordan Peterson's 12 rules are so deeply coded with double meaning. After all, a man establishing a religion that features himself as its prophet and savior will need to do so in secret for many reasons. First, he must keep his activities from being exposed to too much outside scrutiny. Second, he must filter the true believer from the merely curious. Third, he must separate the potential initiates from the doubters and the failures. Fourth, he must maintain plausible deniability for outsiders while drawing the acolyte in ever deeper.

One might well describe Peterson's philosophy as a literal pyramid scheme, albeit one with an All-Seeing Eye watching over it.

Think about the possibility that Peterson's religiosity is not mere flavor, but an indication that he is attempting to establish an actual post-Christian religion. In *12 Rules for Life*, Peterson sneaks in an important concept that will escape most, if not all of his readers. He does this in Rule 2, when he is talking about the spark of the Divine.

We are low-resolution ('kenotic') versions of God. We can make order from chaos—and vice versa—in our way, with our words. So, we may not exactly be God, but we're not exactly nothing, either.

—12 Rules for Life

A superficial reading tends to indicate that Peterson is downplaying the potential godhood of humanity. He seems to be saying that while human beings are made in the image of God, they aren't perfect and they aren't God, but they can model an ethos after Him.

But that isn't what he's saying here. He can't be, because he is again playing the reader false with a misleading definition. The word "kenotic" does not mean "low-resolution." Kenotic is a theological term and a very specific one at that. It refers directly to Jesus Christ and the emptying out of his will in perfect obedience to God's Will. It is a direct and unambiguous reference to the willing self-sacrifice of Christ on the Cross.

In Christian theology, kenosis (Greek: κένωσις, kénōsis, lit. [the act of emptying]) is the 'self-emptying' of Jesus' own will and becoming entirely receptive to God's divine will.

—Wikipedia

In Eastern Orthodoxy, mystics believe that Christ sets the core example of kenosis that his followers are to attempt in humility. Protestants likewise view kenosis as Christ's emptying of himself for the sake of the world. Roman Catholics possess a Papal encyclical *Sempiternus Rex Christus*, which condemns heretics who argue that Christ emptied himself, not of his will, but his divinity, during the Crucifixion.

The deceptive seed Peterson plants here with this revised definition of "kenotic" is the exceedingly heretical and anti-Christian claim that our will is as close to God's will as the universe allows. We are not precisely the God that is described in the Bible, we are not that perfect, Platonic ideal, but our words have divine power nevertheless.

Peterson's frequent citations of the Bible and public agonizing over historical existence of Jesus Christ provides him with the cover he requires to substitute an occult form of universal neo-Taoism for Christianity. As the body of Christ becomes his own body, the language and message of Jesus Christ is transformed into the language and message of Jordan Peterson.

Considering how ignorant of Christian theology Peterson has proven to be, and how inaccurately he represents it, there can be little doubt that he misrepresents Taoism in important ways too. But the important thing is that he treats Christianity as his own personal Trojan Horse, with all manner of occult heresies lurking within.

There are a number of signs that will alert us if Jordanetics begins to transform into a full-blown religious cult. For example, if Peterson's followers start to establish international connections around the world and start founding institutions for the study and propagation of the 12-Rule Path, that will be a reliable indicator that what one fan has told us "feels like a movement" has evolved into an advanced form of Jordanetics that represents a realization of the post-Christian vision originally proposed by Yeats.

As I read it, there are three distinct stages to Yeats' narrative. The first is the age when Christian values were the unchallenged core of Western civilization. This was a vital, flourishing civilization, but now it is over. The second stage is nihilism, both active and passive, occasioned by the loss of these core values. This is the present-day for Yeats and ourselves.

The third stage, which is yet to come, will follow the birth of the "rough beast." Just as the birth of Jesus inaugurated Christian civilization, the rough beast will inaugurate a new pagan civilization. Its core values will be different than Christian values, which, of course, horrifies Christians, who hope to revive their religion. But the new pagan values, unlike Christian ones, will actually be believed, bringing the reign of nihilism to its end and creating a new, vital civilization. For pagans, this is a message of hope.

—Greg Johnson, "Yeats' Pagan *Second Coming*"

Jordanetics, taken at face value, is an observably evil philosophy. It would be considerably worse, and considerably more dangerous, were it to transform into a post-Christian religious cult. But it does not have to do so in order for Jordan Peterson's teachings, training, and psycho-spiritual pathway to prove destructive to individuals and what is left of Western Civilization alike.

Chapter 20

The Global Vision of Jordanetics

I worked on the UN Secretary-General's High Panel for Sustainability Report that was delivered, I believe, in 2013, and rewrote the underlying narrative to strip out most of the ideological claptrap.

—Dr. Jordan Peterson

It may surprise some of his fans to know that Jordan Peterson is a politician at heart. When he was only a teenager, he was already a member of the New Democratic Party, which was created in 1961 from a merger of the Canadian Labour Congress and the Co-operative Commonwealth Federation, which was a populist agrarian party that had been party of the Social Gospel movement, but subsequently evolved into a modern socialist party. The NDP is a secular socialist party that advocates issues such as gay rights, international peace, and environmental stewardship.

Not only that, but in 1971, Peterson even ran for the vice-presidency of the Alberta NDP at the age of 14 and came within 13 votes of winning! His picture was featured in the local newspaper and Peterson himself was quoted as saying, "I won't be happy until I'm elected Prime Minister."

Although Peterson claims to have disavowed his socialist ideology and now describes himself as having evolved beyond all ideologies, he remains an avowed globalist. His primary objective, the mission to which he believes himself to be called to save the world, is to bind the nationalists in order to permit the despoiling of their collective houses. He is committed to this because he wrongly believes that global governance will somehow prevent World War III from occurring.

This is why he is listed as a "sherpa" for one of the Eminent Persons of the United Nations in the U.N. report he co-authored. This is why he attended the 2018 meeting of the Trilateral Commission in Ljubljana, Slovenia.

Jordan Peterson is a wicked and delusional man who has somehow managed to conceal from his misguided followers that he is actively attempting to neuter them in the service of globalist evil. The strange thing is that even when his active involvement in globalist politics is revealed, such as his authorship of *Resilient People, Resilient Planet: A future worth choosing*, his committed fans refuse to even consider the idea that he is involved in politics at all, let alone a deeply political creature.

For example, one of my Darkstream viewers commented that he stopped watching my videos for several months due to my repeated attacks on Peterson. He claimed that I did not realize "that Peterson uses philosophy and psychology better than anyone to liberate both left and right brainwashed sheep, and as a result stays above politics."

The amazing thing is that Peterson's cargo cultists are capable of publicly asserting that Peterson is above politics while he is literally working for the United Nations and relentlessly pushing its globalist line. The truth is that Jordan Peterson is a committed, professional globalist. His most cherished objectives are directly opposed to the survival of America and the West. While some view his rhetoric criticizing globalist institutions such as the United Nations and the European Union as an indication that he is opposed to globalism, they fail to note that he is trying to fix them.

The distance between the typical citizen and the bureaucracy that runs the entire structure has got so great that it's an element of destabilization in and of itself, and so people revert back to, say, nationalistic identities because it's something that they can relate to.

That is not criticism of the existence of the globalist institutions or their objectives, it is merely criticism of their implementation. If someone was trying to fix Nazism, you wouldn't say that he's a Jewish ally. If someone was trying to fix Communism, you wouldn't say that he is a capitalist ally. Jordan Peterson is trying to fix globalism. That necessarily means that he is trying to destroy nationalism, your nation, and your people, which are objectives that he doesn't even hide!

He condemns group identity as pathological. This is an insane condemnation of friends, family, faith, and nation as mental illness! He elevates the individual to the sovereign level at the expense of literally everyone around him. The best way to win the cultural and ideological wars, he insists, is not to fight them, but to preemptively surrender.

I would recommend that people don't do it because the problem with the radical leftists and their damn identity politics is that it's unbelievably pathological. And if you decide to fight that by playing the same game, you think, well, I'll play the same game and then I'll win, it's like, you know, you won't, because by playing the game you lose.

That's the thing about your political opponents is you don't play their damn game, you play a different game. And so you know what I've been trying to encourage people to do is instead of playing the collectivist game—and that would include Alt-Right identity politics—is to play the individualist game and to get their act together.

The best revenge, I would say—you shouldn't be doing it for revenge—but the best revenge against the collective left, of the collectivist leftists is to live a stalwart, meaningful, and high-quality individual life, and that's also the pathway that requires the most responsibility and sacrifice. And, I think is the most honorable and least self-deceptive.

—"Jordan Peterson's Message to Alt-Right Ideologues"

For Peterson to say that it is the honorable and the least self-deceptive path for Americans to simply accept the mass invasion of over 100 million people, to address the largest invasion in all of human history by being noble, and individual, and leading a meaningful life, is such obvious nonsense that it almost defies description.

Imagine if the great men of history had not been pathological group identitarians, but had followed the philosophy of Jordan Peterson's 12-Rule Path:

> *"Ask not what your country can do for you—ask how you can live a stalwart, meaningful, and high-quality individual life."*
>
> —Jordan B. Kennedy

> *"No dumb bastard ever won a war by going out and dying for his country. He won it by living a stalwart, meaningful, and high-quality individual life."*
>
> —Jordan B. Patton

> *"If we play the Britons' game, we lose! Go home, everyone!"*
>
> —Jordan B. Caesar

> *"Dulce et decorum est constantem, excellentem, significantemque propriam vitam vivere."*
>
> —Jordan B. Horace

> *"Moreover, I consider that Carthage must be ignored!"*
>
> —Jordan B. Cicero

Imagine if Jordan Peterson had given that advice to the people of Poland, imagine that he had given that advice to George Washington, or Cincinnatus, or Julius Caesar, or any other great man of history! Literally every one of any note in history rejected the concept of going down to noble individual defeat. Jesus Christ himself summoned 12 disciples to follow him. Even the Buddha, who rejected the world and saw it all as *Maya*, illusion, even he permitted his closest and dearest companions to help him with his life's work as he pursued his search for nirvana.

What Peterson is saying is absolute and utter nonsense, and to sum up my response to his attack on nationalism and group identity, I will present a single quote from a man who understood identity politics much better than anyone. He was a political genius who masterfully managed an extraordinarily difficult situation with a small civic polity that was surrounded and dominated by much larger, more powerful neighbors, was comprised of competing ethnic and religious groups, and the way that he addressed the inevitable identity politics there was not pathological, it was based on reality, and it was absolutely true.

In multiracial societies you don't vote in accordance with your economic interests, you vote in accordance with race and religion.

—Lee Kwan Yew

You must never forget that Jordan Peterson's ultimate goal is to recreate the Tower of Babel. He is more than just a globalist, he is the spiritual descendant of the evil men who sought to challenge God Himself. His insidious campaign against group identity, against nationalism, and against Western civilization is rooted in a literally Satanic desire to raise up a single global government that will rule over all of humanity.

And what Jordan Peterson is attempting to bring about through Jordanetics is the single global religion that will provide the spiritual bulwark for that massive totalitarian edifice, a religion in which he will serve the tripartite role of Messiah, Savior, and Pope.

That may sound crazy and evil, and it is. But Jordan Peterson is crazy and evil! His motivations are very far from hidden. For more than two decades, he has been openly writing about his obsession with the Holocaust and his ambitions to save the world from the next one.

I don't completely understand the driving force behind what I have been working on, although I understand it better now than I used to, three or four years ago, when it was literally driving me crazy. I had been obsessed with the idea of war for three or four years prior to that, often dreaming extremely violent dreams, centered around the theme of destruction. I believe now that my concern with death on a mass scale was intimately tied into my personal life, and that concerns with the meaning of life on a personal level (which arise with the contemplation of death) took a general form for me, which had to do with the value of humanity, and the purpose of life in general....

I hope to describe not only what the problem is (in historical terms), but where a possible solution might lie, and what that solution conceivably could be—and I hope to describe it in a manner that makes its application possible.

—*Maps of Meaning: The Architecture of Belief*

The driving force behind Jordan Peterson, the force that has driven him mad, is not the Spirit of Man. The driving force behind him and his dream of ending war by unifying humanity by severing all human connections to one another is a very different spirit, namely, the evil spirit that Jesus Christ called "the god of this world."

And this is the final and greatest paradox of Jordanetics. The driving force that inspires Jordan Peterson, and has propelled him to such heights of fame and fortune, is the driving force behind the very horrors of history whose recurrences he dreams of preventing through the establishment of his new religion.

Epilogue: Of Wheat and Tares

*People are so tortured by the limitations and constraint of Being that
I am amazed they ever act properly or look beyond themselves at all.*

—Dr. Jordan Peterson

I have seen many Peterson fans, who do not consider themselves to
be deceived by him, talk about their ability to separate the wheat of
his teachings from the chaff. Buried in the midst of the Petersonian
word salad, they perceive individual gems of wisdom, or perhaps a
well-turned phrase, or an intriguing metaphor, and find value in it.
Anything else can be safely dismissed as nonsense

This would be a useful practice if Jordan Peterson's seeds of wisdom
actually consisted of wheat. I hope that by now you have discovered that
Jordan Peterson doesn't plant wheat. To stick with the metaphor, what
he is planting is *Lolium temulentum,* commonly known as poison darnel
and described in the Bible as tare, a species of rye-grass that inhibits
wheat production, but whose plant, in the early stages, is practically
indistinguishable from the wheat plant. It is common to some parts
of the Middle East, and during Roman rule, it was illegal to sow tares
in a wheat field, because discerning the good seed from the bad was
practically impossible.

This was a serious problem, because the tare seed contains a strong
soporific, which was capable of rendering the individual who consumed
it unconscious. This was the basis for one of Jesus Christ's more well-
known parables.

*Another parable put he forth unto them, saying, The kingdom of
heaven is likened unto a man which sowed good seed in his field:
But while men slept, his enemy came and sowed tares among the
wheat, and went his way. But when the blade was sprung up, and
brought forth fruit, then appeared the tares also. So the servants of*

the householder came and said unto him, Sir, didst not thou sow good seed in thy field? from whence then hath it tares? He said unto them, An enemy hath done this. The servants said unto him, Wilt thou then that we go and gather them up? But he said, Nay; lest while ye gather up the tares, ye root up also the wheat with them. Let both grow together until the harvest: and in the time of harvest I will say to the reapers, Gather ye together first the tares, and bind them in bundles to burn them: but gather the wheat into my barn.

—Matthew 13:24-30

Now, if Peterson is sowing a field with no wheat at all, a field that contains nothing besides these sleep-inducing seeds that appear to be healthy wheat during their early development, will there be any chaff to separate and burn in the end? What, exactly, is the true nature of the presumed wheat that you have valued and stored?

If Peterson has planted both wheat and tares together, the only time to separate them comes late, at harvest time, when the deceptive weeds and fruitful wheat are obvious.

The harvest has arrived.

Do you genuinely see anything but poison in Jordan Peterson's words now?

Peterson advises you to be become more self-absorbed, more obedient to authority, less ambitious, less loyal to your friends, less honest, more ruthless, weaker in your faith, and more like Jordan Peterson.

Does that really strike you as a desirable path for your life?

You may think that Peterson has helped others. You may think that he has helped you. But has he really done so? Even if you have managed to clean your room, stand up straight, or pet a cat without getting scratched?

You may consider Jordan Peterson to be a gateway to Christianity. But while there are soldiers who have found Jesus Christ in a foxhole, and people caught up in natural disasters or transportation crises have cried out to God for mercy, that does not mean that war, hurricanes, or sinking ships should be considered evangelical tools. It is entirely possible that there are those who will listen to the insidious philosophy of Jordan Peterson and reject it in favor of a more spiritually healthy alternative. But while this is the best of all the possible consequences that might result, it would not redeem the words and teachings of Peterson himself, nor would it justify his wickedness.

The gnostic nature of Jordanetics is its primary attraction, but therein also lies its inevitable downfall. For the truth will shine for all eternity, while falsehood can survive only as long as it remains safely hidden in the dark.

Appendix A: No Conspiracy

No conspiracy. Get it? No conspiracy. Jewish people are over-represented in positions of competence and authority because, as a group, they have a higher mean IQ.... There is no evidence whatsoever that Ashkenazi Jews are over-represented in any occupations/interests for reasons other than intelligence and the associated effects of intelligence on personality and political belief. Thus, no conspiratorial claims based on ethnic identity need to be given credence.

—Dr. Jordan Peterson

As I promised in the Introduction, I have provided an updated version of my detailed analysis of Jordan Peterson's unprovoked attack on the excessively observant and the science of statistics alike in this appendix. His "No Conspiracy" argument is constructed as follows:

1. One requires a victim and a perpetrator in order to play identity politics.

2. The Far Right has chosen European culture as a victim due to its unrecognized resentment and cowardly and incompetent failure to deal with the world forthrightly, and have incorrectly selected the Jews as perpetrator due to Jewish overrepresentation in positions of authority, competence and influence.

3. Jewish people are overrepresented in positions of competence and authority because, as a group, they have a higher mean IQ.

4. Jews have a mean IQ of 110-115.

5. "40.8% of the 145+ IQ population is Jewish."

6. "There is no evidence whatsoever that Ashkenazi Jews are over-represented in any occupations/interests for reasons other than intelligence and the associated effects of intelligence on personality and political belief. Thus, no conspiratorial claims based on ethnic identity need to be given credence."

Peterson's argument is not merely incorrect, literally every single aspect of it is false. It is so resolutely and demonstrably false that it is highly unlikely for Jordan Peterson to have constructed it in innocence by mistake, even given his self-confessed mathematical limitations. In my opinion, it clearly indicates a malicious intent to deceive his audience and to falsely accuse those he labels "the far right".

My responses to the six points of his argument are as follows:

1. One does not require a victim or a perpetrator in order to play identity politics. One does not need to be aware of identity politics, or even to believe they exist, to find oneself engulfed in them. To quote Lee Kwan Yew, "In multiracial societies, you don't vote in accordance with your economic interests and social interests, you vote in accordance with race and religion." All a society requires is sizable multiracial, multiethnic, or multireligious components and identity politics will inevitably appear once the minority populations become sufficiently numerous or influential.

2. European culture and the European nations of the West are observably and undeniably the victims of mass immigration, of a movement of peoples that is the largest in recorded human history. This is a fact that is no more disputable than the fact that the indigenous American populations were victims of mass immigration in the 16th, 17th, and 18th centuries, or the fact that indigenous Asian populations were victims of immigration,

colonization and imperialism in the 18th, 19th, and 20th centuries. The perpetrators are, by definition, the immigrants as well as those who worked to alter the various laws to permit the entry of large numbers of immigrants.

3. Jews are not overrepresented in positions of competence and authority in the United States because, as a group, they have a higher mean IQ, because a) IQs over 145 do not tend to help, but rather tend to hinder, an individual's ability to attain such positions, and, b) the higher mean IQ postulated is not high enough to compensate for their considerably smaller percentage of the population.

4. Jews do not have a mean IQ of 115. Globally, they appear to have a mean IQ that is an estimated maximum of 103.2. In the USA, where the percentage of the high-IQ Ashkenazim subset makes up a higher percentage of the Jewish population, they have an estimated maximum mean IQ of 105.1. This is perfectly respectable, it simply is not in the 110-115 range.

5. Less than 4 percent of the 145+ IQ population in the USA is Jewish. Not more than 40 percent.

6. Whether they happen to be true or not, conspiratorial claims based on ethnic identity remain a valid potential explanation for Jewish overrepresentation in positions of competence and authority due to Jordan Peterson total failure to prove his case. He is, at best, an inept intellectual disputant, and at worst, an intentional deceiver.

I will now proceed to substantiate my responses to points 3, 4, and 5 in detail. Response 6 follows naturally from them.

On point 3, I observe,

Researchers at the University of Lausanne have determined that there is a linear relationship between intelligence and effective leadership, but this relationship only holds up to an IQ of 120. The association actually reverses at IQs above that level. This is primarily due to the IQ communication gap which prevents effective communication across 2 standard deviations of intelligence, or about 30 IQ points. This negative effect of high IQ is further compounded by the systematic statistical exclusion of the true cognitive elite from the intellectually elite professions.

According to an article entitled "The Inappropriately Excluded" by Michael W. Ferguson published in *The Polymath*, the probability of an individual establishing a career in an intellectually elite profession such as physician, judge, professor, scientist, or CEO, increases in line with IQ to the Mensa level, which comprises the top two percent of the general population. The probability of a successful professional career peaks at 133, then falls about one-third by the time the individual's IQ reaches 140. After that, the probability of success declines rapidly, so that by the time an IQ of 150 is reached, the likelihood of the high-IQ individual successfully pursuing an elite professional career has fallen by 97 percent.

What this means, Ferguson explains, is that the majority of individuals with IQs over 140 have been systematically excluded from the very professions that are responsible for addressing the most important challenges of our time as well as ensuring the functionality of our social, scientific, political and economic institutions. Contra Jordan Peterson's assumption, there actually appears to be a very strong *inverse* relationship between highly intelligent individuals possessing IQs over 140 and success in an academic or professional field.

Therefore, Jordan Peterson's proposed explanation for disproportionate Jewish success in American society is not only incorrect, but ironically, would have demonstrated precisely the opposite of that which he was attempting to prove if it had been correct. The observation that Jews are overrepresented in positions of competence and authority in the United States actually serves as compelling evidence that their mean IQ cannot be uniquely and extraordinarily high.

On point 4, I observe,

The primary and oft-cited source of the 115 mean IQ claim is the 1957 study by Boris Levinson entitled "The Intelligence of Applicants for Admission to Jewish Day Schools" published in *Jewish Social Studies, Vol. 19, No. 3/4* (Jul.–Oct., 1957), pp. 129-140.

In the study, which reported a 114.88 mean IQ for the 2,083 very young students sampled, the author duly noted its intrinsic limitations.

This study is limited to applicants for Day Schools adhering to the principles of the National Commission for Yeshiva Education. This sampling does not claim to represent the entire Jewish school population or even those children attending yeshiva Day Schools with a different educational emphasis.

That 114.88 mean IQ did not represent the entire U.S. Jewish population in 1956 and therefore cannot possibly represent the entire U.S. Jewish population 61 years later. Furthermore, even if it had correctly represented the entire Jewish Ashkenazi population in the USA then, it would not do so now, due to the fact that what had been a relatively pure Ashkenazi population two generations ago is now 44 percent genetically adulterated by the mainstream population due to intermarriage.

The current US population of 5,425,000 Jews is now made up of the following genetic groups:

- 51.6 Ashkenazi
- 40.6 Half-Ashkenazi, Half-European
- 7.8 Sephardic, Mizrahi, and other backgrounds

Remember, it's not the ethnic identity that magically conveys intelligence on an individual, intelligence is primarily a consequence of the individual's genetic ancestry. Even if individuals in the second category consider themselves to be every bit as Jewish as their immigrant Jewish grandparents in a cultural, ethnic, or religious sense, it is not true from

a genetic perspective and the studies on mean Ashkenazi IQ therefore
do not apply to them. I suspect that this is an unintentional focus on
identity instead of genetics on Peterson's part, (an ironic one, given
his attack on identity politics), and it is a mistake that he makes twice.
Now, given that the 107.5 mean Ashkenazi IQ given by Lynn is at least
possibly correct—unlike the false 115 claim which cannot be—and the
102 mean IQ for white Americans, we can more reasonably estimate
the Half-Ashkenazi mean IQ to be halfway between the two population
groups, or 104.8.

Since the non-Ashkenazi Jewish mean IQ is somewhere between 84.2
(if A-IQ=115) and 91 (if A-IQ=107.5) given the reported average IQ
of Israel being 95, this means that the maximum mean IQ of the U.S.
Jewish population is 105.1, 3.1 points higher than the mean White
IQ of 102 but nearly one point below the reported mean East Asian-
American IQ of 106.

On point 5, I observe,

Peterson's assertion that 40.8 percent of the 145+ IQ population in the
USA is Jewish is not merely wrong, it is off by more than an order
of magnitude! First, he ignores the relevant distinctions between the
various minority populations, second, he exaggerates the US Jewish
population by 10 percent, third, he fails to account for the fact that 48.4
percent of that population is either part-Ashkenazi or non-Ashkenazi
and thereby exaggerates their mean IQ, and fourth, he again makes
the mistake of relying upon identity rather than genetics for the White
population. His use of the White, Non-Hispanic population alone
is not correct here, because the White Hispanic population is defined
as being genetically white and therefore cannot be excluded from the
White population numbers.

With a mean IQ of 105.1 and a population of 5,425,000, the
standard distribution curve indicates 21,158 Jews with 145+ IQs in
the United States. In addition to this, the mean IQ of 102 for the

White population of 246,660,710 indicates 517,987 Whites with 145+ IQs, plus 31,913 equally high-IQ Chinese, Japanese, and Koreans, plus another 39,523 Indian-Americans (as opposed to American Indians), resident in the United States. So, the correct ratio of the 145+ IQ population is 21,158 of the 610,581 total.

Jews therefore account for 3.5 percent of the 145+ IQ set in the United States, not 40.8 percent of it. Jordan Peterson was off by more than an order of magnitude!

Note that even if we were to generously allow Peterson his original assertion about the range of mean Jewish IQ, the statistics he presents to defend his conclusion are incorrect. At the highest end of his suggested range, 115, Jews would only account for 123,690 of the 713,113 high-IQ population, or 17.3 percent. At the lower end of 110, the Jewish percentage would necessarily be reduced to less than one-twelfth of the 145+ IQ set in the United States. And just to demonstrate how ridiculous Peterson's statement was, in order to account for 40.8 percent of the U.S. 145+ IQ population, the mean Jewish IQ would need to be 123.4 with 7.5 percent of all U.S. Jews possessing an IQ over 145

This should more than suffice to demonstrate that Jordan Peterson's argument is completely wrong, his conclusion is false, and his public charges of cowardice and "incompetent failure to deal with the world forthrightly" on the part of his critics are not only unfair and incorrect, they appear to be emotional projections of Peterson's own intellectual cowardice and his own failure to deal competently with statistics.

On point 6, I conclude,

I do not know Jordan Peterson, but his incorrect and deceitful arguments, and his unfair and unjustified attacks on his critics, show him to be an inept and integrity-challenged coward who lacks a genuine commitment to the truth. The combination of his sudden success with his observable intellectual ineptitude suggests that he has been elevated by the mainstream media in order to provide a harmless, toothless, and non-Christian alternative to the failed conservative movement of William F. Buckley and the failed neoconservative movement of Bill Kristol and Ben Shapiro.

The Source of the Myth

Just as the journey of a thousand leagues begins with but a single step, even the most widespread and persistent myth can be inspired by a single source. So what was the original basis for Jordan Peterson's assertion that Jews are uniquely intelligent in the first place? Here are a number of the more-often cited sources.

Researchers who study the Ashkenazim agree that the children of Abraham are on top of the IQ chart. Steven Pinker—who lectured on "Jews, Genes, and Intelligence" in 2007—says "their average IQ has been measured at 108-115." Richard Lynn, author of "The Intelligence of American Jews" in 2004, says it is "only" a half-standard higher: 107.5. Henry Harpending, Jason Hardy, and Gregory Cochran, University of Utah authors of the 2005 research report, "Natural History of Ashkenazi Intelligence," state that their subjects, "score .75 to 1.0 standard deviations above the general European average, corresponding to an IQ of 112-115." Charles Murray, in his 2007 essay "Jewish Genius," says "their mean is somewhere in the range of 107-115, with 110 being a plausible compromise." A Jewish average IQ of 115 is 8 points higher than the generally accepted IQ of their closest rivals—Northeast Asians—and approximately 40% higher than the global average IQ of 79.1 calculated by Richard Lynn and Tatu Vanhanen in *IQ and Global Inequity*.

First, you will note the usual definitional switch we've learned to anticipate from Peterson. A subset—the pure Ashkenazi population—is frequently substituted for the full set of Jews with diverse genetic heritages. Second, if one takes the trouble to look up and read the studies that are often referenced but never cited, one is immediately struck by the fact that these studies are a) misrepresented, b) old and outdated, c) almost invariably authored by those with an identity-related bias, and, d) contain samples that are a very small and limited subset of the subset of the set. For example, as previously noted, the primary source of the 115 IQ claim appears to be a 1957 study by Boris Levinson entitled "The Intelligence of Applicants for Admission to Jewish Day Schools" published in *Jewish Social Studies, Vol. 19, No. 3/4* (Jul.–Oct., 1957), pp. 129-140.

Right in the study, which reported a 114.88 mean IQ for the 2,083 students sampled, the author specifically denied it was representational of the Jewish school population in the United States, much less the entire Jewish nation around the world.

Levinson further admits that the students sampled only represented 38 percent of the 5,494 students attending the 16 Day Schools, raising the distinct possibility that the sampled scores were cherry-picked. Now, do you seriously believe that the mean of a partial subset of a wealthy private school subset of a geographically limited subset of a genetic subset is likely to be even *remotely* representational of the mean of the entire global population set? Let alone to almost precisely nail the upper end? This is so utterly absurd on its face that for the more logically inclined, the mere existence of this study should suffice to conclusively refute the myth.

Furthermore, in the study, Levinson refers to a 1956 study by Robert D. North concerning white American fourth-graders from 16 independent private school, and noted the following.

Many of these schools select their pupils on the basis of mental ability and achievement. Because these schools charge tuition fees, most of their pupils come from higher socio-economic levels. These children had a mean IQ of 119.3.

Shall we therefore conclude that the average white American is more intelligent than the average Jew because one very small group of elite private-schooled white Americans outperformed another very small group of elite private-schooled Jews in the 1950s?

Of course not, that would be absolutely nonsensical! *So why do we accept the reverse conclusion?* After all, the samples cited in the studies were not even remotely representative of either population subset then, let alone more than 60 years later.

There are other statistical idiosyncracies that demonstrate the complete irrelevance of these post-WWII IQ studies to current population IQ averages; one study reported that the average IQ of the boys sampled was 112.8 and that of the girls was 113.6. If we are to take these particular IQ studies as definitive, then we must conclude that girls are more intelligent than boys, all other subsequent studies and observations to the contrary.

There are many other reasons to be dubious of what increasingly appears to be a statistical myth of uniquely high Jewish intelligence. Consider Israel, for example. It is a successful quasi-European society, superior in nearly all respects to the lower-IQ Arab societies surrounding it, but it is no more technologically advanced or socio-economically successful than most Western or East Asian societies, and it remains economically dependent upon regular handouts from Germany and the USA. Even after 70 years, despite many impressive accomplishments and advancements, it is not exactly the advanced Wakanda in the Middle East that one would expect a society constructed by such a uniquely intelligent population to be. An application of Ockham's Razor suggests that this is because it is not.

Moreover, where was this disproportional high-IQ success in Roman times, in the Middle Ages and in the Renaissance? Where was it in the Napoleonic era? Why has what Peterson describes as "overrepresentation in positions of competence and authority" only appeared after a sufficient degree of broad societal influence in specific societies such as the United States and Israel has been obtained? And how did so many European nations manage to observably benefit after they supposedly reduced the average IQ of their populations as a result of the various historical expulsions?

The good news for those who are interested in the truth, whatever it happens to be, is that despite the reproducibility crisis in scientistry, the relentless advancement of scientage means it is increasingly difficult to utilize dishonest citations of biased studies of limited relevance from six decades ago to deceive the general public. The advancement of genetic science and the confirmed links between genetics and intelligence can be safely expected to scientifically explode an outdated and self-serving myth that has been relentlessly pushed upon the unsuspecting American public along with related myths such as the Zeroth Amendment, "a nation of immigrants", "the melting pot", and "Judeo-Christianity".

Regardless of what the actual facts of the matter turn out to be, they will eventually be known and they will eventually be scientifically confirmed beyond the possibility of reasonable dispute. If the skeptics are correct and this assertion of uniquely high IQ turns out to be a myth, then we can safely expect to see the link that Jordan Peterson and others have made between high average IQ and societal success to be downplayed, just as Ivy League admissions officers are already attempting to downplay the importance of test scores and intellectual merit in the admissions processes of the elite universities.

In conclusion, it is perhaps worth noting that at least one IQ expert has said that my criticism of the position Peterson publicly espouses is not unfounded. John Fuerst of the Ulster Institute was following the discussion of the matter on my blog and left the following comment there.

I more or less agree with Vox. I collaborate with Richard Lynn and I am familiar with the literature and most of the studies (both reported and not). As for Israel, on international tests, Hebrew speakers (Jews) score around the level of White Europeans, while Arab speakers score around that of other Middle Easterners (around 1+ standard deviation below the European White mean). See, for example, "Why Israel does poorly in the PISA exams—perceptions versus reality (2017)", and the Taub Centers' "State of the nation picture (2014/2017)" reports.

For example, the non-Haredi Jewish PISA 2012 math average was 489 (SD ~93), for White Americans for the same year it was 506 (SD 83). For Israel and the US as a whole, the means and SDs were, respectively, 481 (SD 90) and 466 (SD 105).

There is year to year variability. But it is safe to say that on international math, reading, and science exams, Israeli Jews do no better than Whites in typical Western countries. Note, these figures exclude most Haredi Jews who both do rather poor on exams (see the Taub Center's reports) and who are around 80% Ashk. Thus, the testing samples tend to be less Ashk than the general population, but the excluded Ashk are substantially less proficient than average.)

Thus, as Vox notes, if one argues that Ashk Israeli come in at around 115, one has to maintain that non-Ashk Jews come in around 85. Yet, this latter conjecture is inconsistent with the variance among Jews and, more notably, the national scores at the 98th percentile, a point which can be shown quantitatively.

Appendix B: 12 Questions for Jordan Peterson

The truth is something that burns, it burns off deadwood and people don't like having their deadwood burnt off because they're 95 percent deadwood

—Dr. Jordan Peterson

I am frequently asked by people planning to attend a Jordan Peterson lecture for suggestions concerning a question they can ask him if they are given the opportunity to do so in a Q&A session. So, here are twelve questions to which the answers he provides may serve to burn off a little of the old deadwood.

1. Since you have said that Jewish possession of a mean IQ 10 to 15 points above the average is responsible for their societal success in the United States, is it correct to conclude that it is the African-American mean IQ being 15 points below the average that is responsible for their societal failure there?

2. What is the longest you have ever gone without sleep?

3. Do you still feel that you will never be happy until you are elected Prime Minister? Have you ever known happiness or joy?

4. Have you ever taken part in an occult or esoteric ritual?

5. Given that you are an outspoken fan of Aleksandr Solzhenitsyn, would you be willing to write an introduction to the English translation of his book *200 Years Together*?

6. Did you ever experience physical or sexual abuse as a minor?

7. You have said that you consider group identity to be dangerous and pathological. Do you consider yourself to be a Canadian?

8. As a professional psychologist, how would you describe your mental illness in clinical terms?

9. Have you ever been baptized as an adult in the Name of the Father, the Son, and the Holy Spirit?

10. Do you believe that you are destined to save humanity from destroying itself? If so, how would you identify the force or Being that has chosen you to do so?

11. Have you ever been professionally diagnosed as a sociopath or a schizophrenic?

12. What will you call yourself as the head of this post-Christian religion of the 12-Rule Path of Balance for which you are presently proselytizing? The Para-Pope of Psycho-Spiritualism? The Tetrarch of Therapeutic Neo-Thelema? The Archprophet of the Post-Adamic Apotheosis?

Appendix C: 12 Real Rules for Life

All is vanity. What is it that we must bestow our care and diligence upon? Even upon this only: that our minds and wills be just; that our actions be charitable; that our speech be never deceitful, and that our understanding be not subject to error; that our inclination be always set to embrace whatsoever shall happen unto us.

—Marcus Aurelius

In light of my criticism and open contempt for Jordan Peterson's 12 rules, on both the superficial and secret levels, I am occasionally asked to provide 12 alternative rules that would prove more effective for the individual seeking to improve his life. After a modicum of reflection, these are my suggestions drawn from 50 years of various successes and failures.

1. **Embrace the iron.** Lifting weights will not only help you stand up straight, it will make you stronger, healthier, and more confident. The iron teaches the weak to be strong and it teaches the strong to be humble.

2. **Take the wheel.** You are the ultimate architect of your own decisions and actions. Even if you were dealt a bad card by life, even if your genetics are inferior, your upbringing was terrible, and your instincts are suboptimal, you are the only one who can improve yourself. You are driving and only you can determine the destination.

3. **Be the friend that you want to have.** Smiles are contagious. Loyalty inspires loyalty. Stand by those who stand by you. Give every friend who fails you a second chance. Only abandon those who have repeatedly proven they cannot be trusted and do not wish you well.

4. **Envision perfection and pursue excellence.** You will never achieve perfection. But if you envision it and you strive for it, you may well achieve success, and perhaps even excellence.

5. **Put a ring on it.** Marriage is the manifestation of love. Children are the manifestation of hope. Raising a family to serve as the foundation of future generations is how Man rebels against an uncaring universe, a fallen world, and the spirits of despair and destruction. Yes, there are real risks, especially in the current social and legal environment. But they are well worth taking nevertheless.

6. **Set your face against evil.** You will encounter evil within and evil without on a daily basis. Stand against all of it, without fear, without hesitation, and without remorse. And when you fail, when you give into temptation, when you are defeated, regroup, repent, and rise again.

7. **Do what is right.** Learn to listen to the still, small voice of conscience. Do what you know to be right, not what you can rationalize, justify, or excuse. If you have to talk yourself into something, then you probably already know in your heart of hearts that you are doing the wrong thing.

8. **Tell the truth in kindness.** It is too hard and too exhausting to spend all your mental energies trying to keep track of an ever-growing multitude of exaggerations, false narratives, self-serving spins, and outright lies. Just tell the truth, as you best understand it, without taking pride in it or using it to hurt others.

9. **Learn the easy way.** You will always encounter those who are stronger, smarter, and more successful than you are. Rather than envying them or attempting to tear them down to make yourself feel better, do your best to learn from them and apply those lessons to your own life. It is considerably easier and more efficient to learn from the mistakes of others than it is to make all of those same mistakes yourself.

10. **Believe the mirror.** The most reliably self-destructive mistake you can make is to lie to yourself about who, what, and where you are, because doing so precludes any real self-improvement. Be ruthless with your self-assessments, without wallowing in self-pity or despair.

11. **Get back on the horse.** Perseverance is one of the most important skills a man can develop. There is absolutely no substitute for the confidence and the courage that comes from the certain knowledge that you will get up again after an opponent, or life, knocks you down.

12. **Find a best friend.** Dogs teach us many things, perhaps the most important of which is what unconditional love is. No matter how rich and successful a man may be, there is no life that the addition of a dog would not considerably improve. And yes, all dogs go to Heaven, obviously, because Heaven would not be paradise without them.

THE END

CASTALIA HOUSE

Non-Fiction
Ship of Fools by C. R. Hallpike
4D Warfare by Jack Posobiec
The Last Closet by Moira Greyland
The Nine Laws by Ivan Throne
A History of Strategy by Martin van Creveld
Compost Everything by David the Good
Grow or Die by David the Good
Push the Zone by David the Good

Fiction
Turned Earth: a Jack Broccoli Novel by David the Good
The Missionaries by Owen Stanley
The Promethean by Owen Stanley
An Equation of Almost Infinite Complexity by J. Mulrooney
Brings the Lightning by Peter Grant
Rocky Mountain Retribution by Peter Grant
Six Expressions of Death by Mojo Mori
Loki's Child by Fenris Wulf
Hitler in Hell by Martin van Creveld

Military Science Fiction
There Will Be War Volumes I and II ed. Jerry Pournelle
Riding the Red Horse Volume 1 ed. Tom Kratman and Vox Day
Starship Liberator by David VanDyke and B.V. Larson
Battleship Indomitable by David VanDyke and B.V. Larson

Science Fiction
CTRL-ALT REVOLT! by Nick Cole
Soda Pop Soldier by Nick Cole
Pop Kult Warrior by Nick Cole
City Beyond Time by John C. Wright
Superluminary by John C. Wright
Back From the Dead by Rolf Nelson

Fantasy
Iron Chamber of Memory by John C. Wright
The Green Knight's Squire by John C. Wright
The Book of Feasts & Seasons by John C. Wright

Lightning Source UK Ltd.
Milton Keynes UK
UKHW041313171218
334146UK00001B/211/P